World University Library

The World University Library is an international series
of books, each of which has been specially commissioned.
The authors are leading scientists and scholars from all over
the world who, in an age of increasing specialisation, see the
need for a broad, up-to-date presentation of their subject.
The aim is to provide authoritative introductory books for
university students which will be of interest also to the general
reader. The series is published in Britain, France, Germany,
Holland, Italy, Spain, Sweden and the United States.

Frontispiece. Women workers helping to construct
the Durgapur Steelworks in India.

Jagdish Bhagwati

The Economics of Underdeveloped Countries.

World University Library

McGraw-Hill Book Company
New York Toronto

To my parents

© Jagdish Bhagwati 1966
Library of Congress Catalog Card Number: 64–66179
Filmset by BAS Printers Limited, Wallop, Hampshire, England
printed by
Officine Grafiche Arnoldo Mondadori, Verona, Italy

Contents

PART ONE

The incidence of squalor

A village scene in Ethiopia–
a woman cooking pancakes of
millet and water, a typical Ethiopian
food. The improvement of food habits
due to poverty is a basic health problem
in the underdeveloped countries.

1 Poverty and income distribution

The world we live in presents a picture of appalling contrasts. While a few countries are immensely prosperous, nearly two-thirds of the population of the world subsists on sub-standard incomes. Illiteracy, bad housing, lack of medical care and malnutrition are prevalent throughout most of Asia, Africa, the Middle East and Latin America. These facts can no longer be ignored. Indeed they have come to dominate intellectual thought and political action to an unprecedented degree in our time.

The poor nations are variously described as 'backward', 'underdeveloped' and 'developing'. The choice of word depends largely on the sensitivity of the audience and the sensibility of the analyst. Ironically, it is the most emotive word, 'backward', that gets closest to the essence of their problems.

Underdeveloped in what sense?

These countries have fallen behind in the race for higher incomes. They also happen to be underdeveloped in relation to their potential income levels. But while it is significant to argue that some countries are poorer than others, it is trivial to claim that each country could become richer than it is now. It is worth setting out the reasons why.

1 Even if expansion depended on the availability of natural resources, perhaps no nation is so destitute of them as to have no potential for expanding its level of income. It is possible, of course, to imagine areas with dim economic prospects. Kuwait without oil would perhaps have had to reconcile itself to permanently low subsistence, relieved only by migration to better-endowed, adjacent areas. Few nations, however, fall into this pattern. Historically, nations seem to have a tendency to become economically viable and remain so. While regions within nations may be beyond the range of worthwhile exploitation, this is rarely true of nations as a whole.

2 In any event, countries are *not* totally dependent on their natural resources. The rise of Britain as an industrial power in the

Table 1. *Gross national product per capita, mid-1950's* (*U.S. dollars*).
'Gross' means that no deduction is made for the depreciation of the capital
stock in producing the national product. National product
is equivalent to national income.

Rank	Value	Country	Rank	Value	Country
1	2,343	United States	26	442	Italy
2	1,667	Canada	27	387	Hungary
3	1,249	New Zealand	28	381	Union of S. Africa
4	1,229	Switzerland	29·5	374	Argentina
5	1,215	Australia	29·5	374	Cyprus
6	1,194	Luxembourg	31	361	Cuba
7	1,165	Sweden	32	356	Surinam
8	1,146	Iceland	33	350	Panama
9	1,046	France	34	330	Colombia
10	1,015	Belgium	35	320	Rumania
11	998	United Kingdom	36	311	Br. Guiana
12	969	Norway	37	307	Costa Rica
13	941	Finland	38·5	298	Malaya
14	913	Denmark	38·5	298	Br. N. Borneo
15·5	762	West Germany	40	297	Yugoslavia
15·5	762	Venezuela	41	292	Hong Kong
17	708	Netherlands	42	285	Bulgaria
18	682	U.S.S.R.	43	276	Turkey
19	569	Uruguay	44	269	Lebanon
20	543	Czechoslovakia	45	265	Jamaica
21	540	Israel	46	262	Brazil
22	532	Austria	47·5	254	Nicaragua
23	511	Puerto Rico	47·5	254	Spain
24	509	Ireland	49	244	El Salvador
25	468	Poland	50	240	Japan

Rank	Value	Country	Rank	Value	Country
51	239	Greece	74	103	Liberia
52	205	Dominican Republic	75	102	Taiwan
53	204	Ecuador	77	100	Thailand
54·5	201	Portugal	77	100	Iran
54·5	201	Philippines	77	100	Sudan
56	195	Iraq	79	98	Belgian Congo
57	187	Mexico	80	96	Jordan
58	180	Chile	81	90	Libya
59	179	Guatemala	82	80	S. Korea
60	176	Algeria	83	75	Haiti
61	166	Saudi Arabia	84	72	India
62	159	Morocco	85·5	70	Nigeria
63	140	Peru	85·5	70	Port. Africa
64	137	Honduras	87	66	Bolivia
65	135	Ghana	88	61	Br. E. Africa
66	134	Federation of Rhodesia and Nyasaland	89·5	58	Fr. W. Africa
67·5	133	S. Vietnam	89·5	58	Fr. Equatorial Africa
67·5	133	Egypt	91·5	56	Pakistan
69	131	Tunisia	91·5	56	China
70	127	Indonesia	93·5	54	Afghanistan
71	122	Ceylon	93·5	54	Ethiopia
72	111	Syria	95	52	Burma
73	108	Paraguay	96	40	Nepal

late eighteenth century was linked with the growth of the Lancashire textiles industry; but Britain imported the raw cotton. Japan's impressive blast furnaces today process imported ore. Trade thus opens up the possibility of breaking through the constraints imposed by natural resources and links growth more intimately to population and capital accumulation – both of which leave a continuing potential for economic expansion.

3 Countries are not limited to their own resources: capital, skilled labour and technical knowledge move across national frontiers.

4 The scientific revolution has also finally rendered meaningless the idea of a nation with no potential for expansion. The growth of science has steadily advanced the prospects for material improvement: techniques for locating mineral resources, improving crops and increasing production from given materials, for example, are continuously being devised. This process will undoubtedly continue.

The significant fact, therefore, is *not* the truism that each country can do better than it does, but the low income level of many countries – *both* in itself *and* relative to the high incomes of the few others. Backwardness is defined in relation to the advanced countries; underdevelopment obtains in contrast to the developed countries.

Measuring and comparing national incomes

It is possible to attempt a quantitative assessment of the income levels reached by different nations and hence of their relative positions. However, a few tricky problems have to be tackled before this can be done.

To compute the income of a nation, the different commodities produced by it have to be reduced to a single number. This means that one must devise a way of reducing all outputs to an equivalent amount of a single commodity. The economist immediately recognises this problem as that of choosing a *price structure* (implying a set of conversion ratios) which can be used to estimate national income. If, for instance, an apple costs twice as much as a pear, it is equivalent to two pears. Each commodity or service can thus be converted into equivalent pears and (through the choice of the pear price) into national income measured in currency units.

Some of the most difficult aspects of international comparisons of incomes are due to this necessity to reduce multi-dimensional information to a single-dimensional figure. For instance, if one wishes to compare the Lebanese real income with the Venezuelan, which of the two price structures is one to select? Even when the choice is confined to the current Lebanese and Venezuelan price structures, there may be a contradiction in the ranking of the two countries. Venezuelan prices may reveal Lebanon to be richer; Lebanese prices may reveal the opposite. The use of either country's prices to calculate the other's income may also make nonsense of the comparison when the two countries have little in common: the use of the price-ratio between furs and refrigerators in Siberia to evaluate the income of the Sahara would be a good example.

International comparisons of income are frequently vitiated also by more mundane considerations, such as differences in measurement conventions. The Soviet Union, for instance, prefers to omit most services from its income estimates since ideology regards them as 'unproductive'; whereas the United States (and other 'capitalist' nations) count them in.

Distortions in comparison may also be produced by differences in economic organisation. Self-driving motorists do not figure in the calculations but chauffeurs do: a system that produced a large share of the former would therefore have its income relatively underestimated.

National income statisticians, however, have been undeterred by these and other difficulties. Indeed, estimates of international comparisons of income are available for some recent years. But before these are produced and used, two points must be made.

1 We must realise that income *originating* in a country may be different from that *accruing* to it. The former corresponds to domestic production. The latter differs from it because a country's

Figure 1. *Underdeveloped countries.* Countries with per capita G.N.P. *below* the world mean ($200 calculated from available statistics for 96 countries) range from Nepal to Iraq and are easily classified as underdeveloped. To these, yet other low-income countries are usually added, ranging from the Philippines to

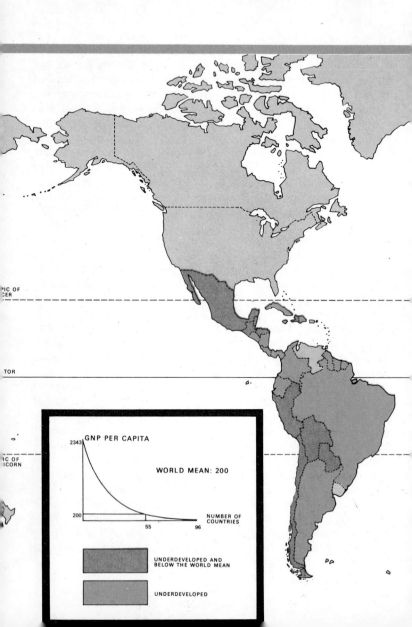

Argentina, and also classified as underdeveloped. Note that nearly all of these countries lie in Asia, Africa, the Middle East and Latin America, and that many of them also lie between the tropics of Cancer and Capricorn.

nationals may earn income abroad whereas domestic income may be earned by foreigners. The national income figures produced here refer to the latter concept. In some cases this may well be a distinction of considerable significance: the income accruing to India and China, but originating abroad – and resulting in remittances from overseas Indians and Chinese, for instance – is not entirely negligible, and in the case of Nepal such income is quite impressive.

2 While aggregate income by itself does reflect the extent to which resources have been harnessed for the use of a country, it does not capture the extra dimension imposed by international differences in the numbers that must subsist on these incomes. The usual way out of this difficulty is to compute national income on a per capita basis. But even this method has its limitations. Population is *not* a homogeneous mass: a nation with a higher ratio of non-adults may be in a happier situation than another with identical per capita income. (Differences in per capita incomes may also affect the proportion of income that has to be allocated merely to 'maintain' the country: for example, a greater population density *may* affect the requirements for defence expenditure and change the share of the total income that accrues to other uses directly increasing economic well-being.)

The distribution of world income

Despite these caveats, it is instructive to examine the broad picture that emerges from available estimates of national per capita incomes. Table 1 presents these statistics for ninety-six countries for the mid-1950's. This coverage is not exhaustive, as many underdeveloped areas – such as Togoland, Liberia, Somalia, Ghana, Swaziland, Mongolia, Sarawak and Yemen – are missing from the table because reliable estimates are not available. In these instances, 'rougher' estimates have been used to produce a nearly complete world picture (see figure 1). A few interesting conclusions can be drawn.

1 Approximately two-thirds of the world's population (inhabiting the areas shown in dark brown in figure 1) has a per capita income below the world mean. The highest per capita income is nearly 600 times greater than the lowest!

2 The selection of countries to be classified as underdeveloped is necessarily arbitrary. Those with per capita incomes below the world mean seem to qualify without difficulty. To these have also been added the countries ranking 29·5 to 54·5 in table 1 (shown in pale brown in figure 1). The uppermost country in the resulting group of underdeveloped countries, Argentina, has a per capita income less than one-sixth that of the United States. This list of underdeveloped countries is in conformity with the general notions of the division of the world into rich and poor nations.

3 The majority of nations with per capita incomes below the world average belong to Asia, the Near East, Africa and Latin America. Asia is the most depressed area, trailing behind Africa, the Near East and Latin America in that order.

4 Many of the underdeveloped countries also lie in the tropical and semi-tropical zones. This is almost certainly fortuitous. It is easy to be tempted into a climatic explanation of underdevelopment and there is perhaps some truth in such a point of view: enervating heat, for instance, can have a disastrous effect on human industriousness; fierce monsoons may erode the soil and make life hazardous in equatorial regions. But too much can be made of such arguments. After all, climate is subject to human manipulation in numerous ways: refrigeration and air-conditioning, for instance, reduce the rigours of heat, The historic evolution of a world split into rich and poor areas is too complex a phenomenon to be explained in any simple terms.

Minimum income levels: an extra dimension

The per capita income statistics, however, lack an important dimension. What lends poignancy to the situation in which the underdeveloped countries find themselves is not merely their

Not only are underdeveloped countries poor as a whole: such wealth as there is is unevenly distributed, so that the visitor is constantly struck by the contrast between luxury and squalor. *Below*: a view of the affluent Avenida Copacabana in Rio de Janeiro and *right*, less than a mile away, one of Rio's typical favelas which 'house' 10% of the city's inhabitants, mostly illiterate and unemployed.

poverty but also its uneven distribution among their citizens. The lowest incomes are well below the average per capita incomes. Hence the level of poverty that prevails in the underdeveloped areas is more striking than the per capita incomes would indicate.

Since their minimum incomes are abysmally small, similar disparities in income between different groups ought also to appear *more* intolerable in the underdeveloped regions. This, indeed, is the case. Inequalities hit the eye forcefully in many of the poorer countries. Visits to these areas are like a trip in a time-machine. Air-conditioned Cadillacs can be seen with bullock-carts. Luxurious houses contrast with peasant hovels.

Are the inequalities in fact greater in the underdeveloped countries, as some analysts have claimed? It is difficult to give a convincing answer either way. Statistics on income distribution in poorer countries hardly exist. What is known, however, from the limited documentation available is not likely to bear out the contention that *wide* differences in income-inequality obtain between countries.

For some of the less backward countries, which differ among themselves in their per capita income, economists have estimates of the distribution of income. Their method consists in ranking households or individual earners by their incomes. These are then divided into 'percentiles'. For instance, if the ranked households are split into ten equal sets from top to bottom, these are known as decile groups. The shares in total income accruing to each of the deciles are then estimated. It is customary to compare the share going to the uppermost decile with that of the lowest. Alternatively, the share of income that accrues to the topmost decile – the richest 10% – is taken by itself. Unfortunately, the information on these questions is limited. Yet the few observations that have been made (for the United States, Britain, Canada, Sweden, Puerto Rico, Ceylon and El Salvador) *suggest* that the share going to the uppermost decile may be less in the advanced countries.

Another statistical measure of income-inequality, which is more

Figure 2. *Lorenz curves of income distribution.* This illustration
shows a statistical method of comparing income-inequalities
within different countries. O A represents percentages of earners,
A B the corresponding percentages of income accruing
to these earners. O B represents an ideal state of complete income equality.
While income inequality varies, from country to country,
the differences follow no pattern and are not pronounced.

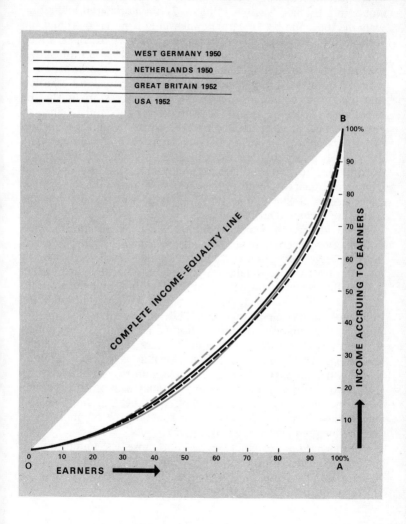

sophisticated, relies on what is known as the Lorenz curve technique. In a triangle (such as in figure 2), the horizontal line represents the total number of earners (measured from O to A) and the vertical line their total income (measured from A to B). It is then possible to draw a curve (joining O and B): each point on it shows the proportion of total income accruing to a certain proportion of earners. Point B, for instance, contains the trivial information that the entire income accrues to all earners. Less obviously, the hypotenuse (OB) represents a situation of complete income equality since, at each point on it, the corresponding proportion of earners enjoys an identical proportion of total income. Any deviation from the hypotenuse will thus imply an *unequal* income distribution. It is natural, therefore, to measure the degree of income-inequality in terms of the *deviation* between the hypotenuse and the curved line (connecting O and B) which represents the prevailing income distribution.

The evidence on which economists can judge international differences in income-inequality, as measured by this index, is unfortunately very limited. Differences do exist between the few countries with estimates. At the same time, they are neither systematic nor large enough to sustain anything but the cautious conclusion that there appear to be no striking international differences in income-inequalities. This may partly be a statistical illusion. The reliability of information varies greatly from country to country. The pattern of inequality may shift with the choice of another earning unit (e.g. households may give results different from individual earners); and for each country, as some sociologists have validly argued, a different unit may be more appropriate. None the less, one can legitimately conclude that the available information leaves an impression of some degree of similarity in income-inequalities between countries.

But this need not cause any concern to those who find inequality in the underdeveloped countries particularly offensive. It is difficult not to sympathise with the view that poverty is to be tolerated only if it is shared by all.

2 Standards of living

In popular analyses of underdeveloped countries, the question of the *standard of living* is frequently introduced. It is also generally identified with the concept of *national income*. Such an identification, however, is incorrect and often leads to serious confusion: the two notions are quite distinct.

Income (accruing) measures the resources available for use to the community. The *standard of living*, on the other hand, falls short of income in so far as it refers only to that part of it which is allocated to current consumption; it also refers to certain extra dimensions such as the expectancy of life, the availability of doctors per capita, conditions of employment and similar indicators of the way in which human existence is conditioned and enriched.

The distinction between income and current consumption (which is included in the standard of living) is of some significance. It is also the difference most easily overlooked. Countries ranked according to per capita incomes are unlikely to remain in the same relative positions if ranked according to consumption per capita. There are two rather different types of reason for this.

1 Nations have to spend varying parts of their incomes merely to 'preserve' themselves. Such use of national income does not contribute directly to the standard of living but merely makes its enjoyment possible. Defence expenditure is a good illustration, though it is not the only one. (And yet, such expenditures must not be thought of as *wholly* irrelevant to the notion of living standards. With defence outlays, for instance, it is possible that they help to maintain high levels of employment, income and consumption in developed economies that might otherwise be threatened by depression.)

Such expenditures vary widely from country to country. Defence expenditure, for example, varies significantly as a proportion of income both between and within the high-income and low-income groups (see figure 3).

2 Such international differences spring also from the different provisions that societies make, consciously or unwittingly, for the future. Countries set aside some fraction of their current national

Figure 3. *Defence expenditure as a percentage of gross domestic product, 1957–9 average.* There is a wide variation in these percentages from one country to another. Moreover, these differences bear no relation to whether a country is in the high-income or the low-income group.

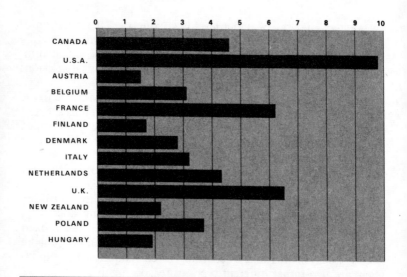

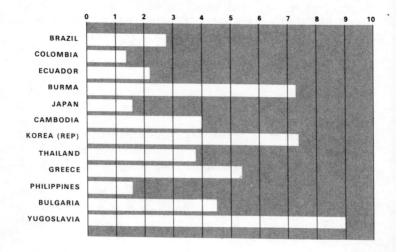

Figure 4. *Fixed capital formation as a proportion of gross national product, 1958.* Since national production may be used for investment or for consumption, higher rates of investment imply that correspondingly less is available for consumption. Hence the observed difference in rates of investment between countries influence international differences in consumption levels.

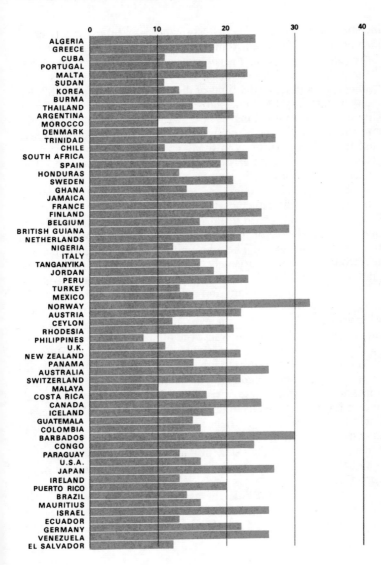

An undernourished child in the Cauca Valley of Colombia, where the land is rich but the people are poor. Life expectancy – one of the indicators of the standard of living – may vary by as much as thirty-five years between a developed and an underdeveloped country. Similar contrasts exist in rates for infant mortality: in Colombia, for instance, 100 children out of every 1,000 born die before they are twelve months old, in the U.S., 25.

incomes as investments which contribute to future increases in income levels. More jam tomorrow is frequently in conflict with more jam today. Focus on *current* consumption levels may thus distort the true relative positions of different countries. For instance, in popular evaluations of the performance of the U.S.S.R., many writers forget to make allowances for the fact that the Soviet Union has been ploughing back a sizeable fraction of its income into investments in the heavy industry sector to provide a massive base for *future* expansions in living standards. The point is quite general: countries differ widely among themselves in their allocation of income to investments (see figure 4).

In addition to consumption levels, there are a number of notions which are neither part of current income nor linked to it. These fall into two broad groups. On the one hand, there are such indices as the degree of freedom, of social mobility, of equality of opportunity and so on. These are more or less immeasurable and the economist, not surprisingly, leaves them out of his statistical analysis. On the other hand, there are certain other variables, which are equally important and which *can* be brought within the range of reasonable quantitative assessment. Among the most widely used indicators are the expectation of life at various ages, the infant mortality rate, literacy, the number of hospital beds per 1,000 population and the availability of jobs and of schooling.

Many of these variables tend to be correlated with the world pattern of per capita incomes. This is not always as puzzling as it appears. Sometimes these variables reflect current income levels and/or the level of past incomes: hospital facilities, for instance, are likely to be greater in the richer countries. At times, the relation may be significant because the level of per capita income itself is a function of the variable listed: for instance, a higher literacy rate may be one of the key factors contributing to a higher level of per capita income.

Whatever the causal link, the association of low per capita in-incomes with a sub-standard performance in terms of some critical components of the standard of living is evident. For instance, the

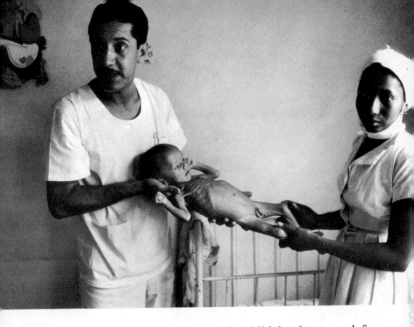

expectation of life of a new-born male child is above, and frequently well above, sixty years in the advanced countries such as the United States, U.K., France, Belgium, Canada, Sweden, U.S.S.R., the Netherlands, Italy, Israel, Austria, East and West Germany and Norway. In contrast, when the corresponding life-expectancy in underdeveloped countries has been observed, it has generally varied between twenty-five and fifty-five: India, Mauritius, Ghana, Egypt, Turkey, Haiti, Guatemala, El Salvador, Cambodia and Costa Rica provide excellent illustrations.

Or consider the world distribution of infant mortality. The number of infant deaths per 1,000 live births are available for ninety-six countries. These figures, mainly for 1955, are neither totally accurate nor totally comparable. They are based on incomplete information or on indirect evidence (e.g. the date of registration rather than the date of actual birth may be used). None the less, the evidence is useful for drawing broad conclusions. It is clear that the bulk of the reporting countries with a mortality rate greater than 60·0 per 1,000 are among the underdeveloped countries (see figure 5); few advanced countries fall into this category.

Figure 5. *Infant mortality (infant deaths per 1,000 live births) and underdevelopment, several dates but generally 1950's.* Infant mortality *above* the world mean (calculated from the available statistics of 96 countries) is found almost exclusively in the underdeveloped

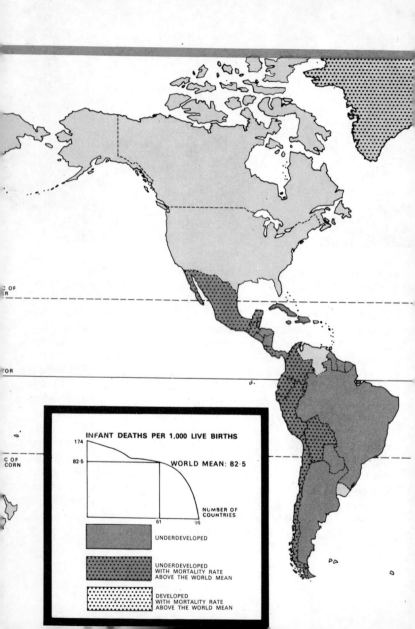

INFANT DEATHS PER 1,000 LIVE BIRTHS

174

82·5

WORLD MEAN: 82·5

NUMBER OF COUNTRIES

61   96

UNDERDEVELOPED

UNDERDEVELOPED
WITH MORTALITY RATE
ABOVE THE WORLD MEAN

DEVELOPED
WITH MORTALITY RATE
ABOVE THE WORLD MEAN

countries. Unfortunately, statistics for some large,
underdeveloped regions – China, parts of Africa and some parts
of the Middle East – are not available. It is likely however
that the infant mortality rates in these areas are also very high.

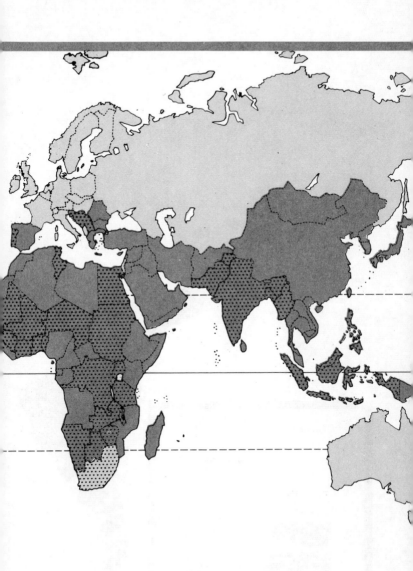

Figure 6. *Availability of physicians and dentists (per 100,000 population) and underdevelopment, generally early 1950's.* Availability *below* the world mean (calculated from the available statistics of 122 countries) is found almost exclusively in the underdeveloped

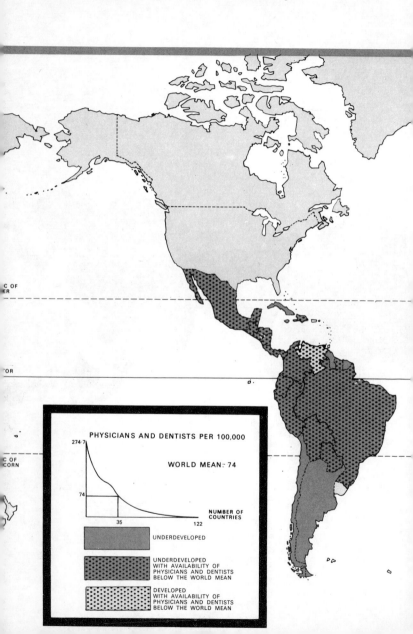

PHYSICIANS AND DENTISTS PER 100,000

274·7

WORLD MEAN: 74

74

35   122

NUMBER OF
COUNTRIES

UNDERDEVELOPED

UNDERDEVELOPED
WITH AVAILABILITY OF
PHYSICIANS AND DENTISTS
BELOW THE WORLD MEAN

DEVELOPED
WITH AVAILABILITY OF
PHYSICIANS AND DENTISTS
BELOW THE WORLD MEAN

countries. Moreover, nearly all the underdeveloped countries
have a lower availability of physicians and dentists than the
advanced countries. The quality of these services is also
certainly lower in the underdeveloped areas.

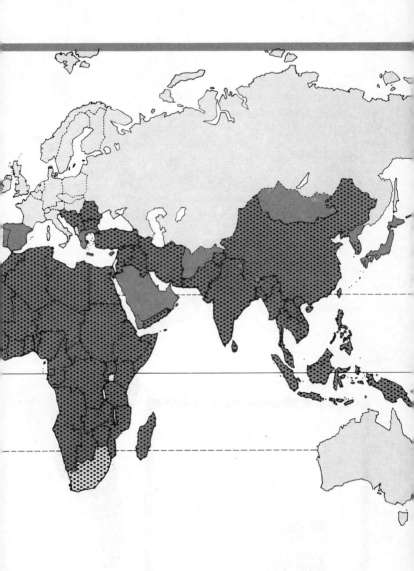

Figure 7. *Literacy rate (percentage of adults literate) and underdevelopment, generally around 1950.* Literacy rates *below* the world mean (calculated from the available statistics of 136 countries) are found almost

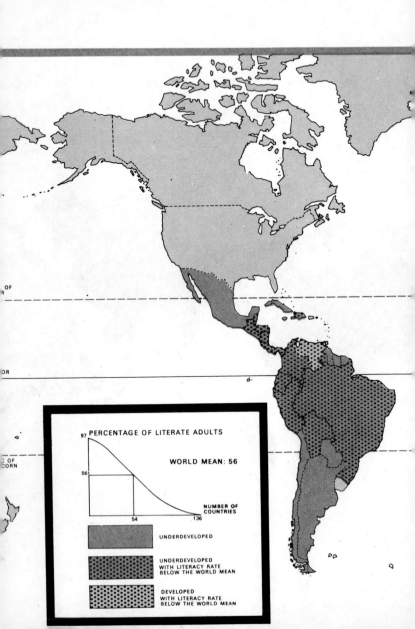

PERCENTAGE OF LITERATE ADULTS

97

WORLD MEAN: 56

56

NUMBER OF COUNTRIES

54   136

UNDERDEVELOPED

UNDERDEVELOPED WITH LITERACY RATE BELOW THE WORLD MEAN

DEVELOPED WITH LITERACY RATE BELOW THE WORLD MEAN

entirely in the underdeveloped countries. Moreover, nearly all the underdeveloped countries have a lower literacy rate than the advanced countries.

The link between low per capita income and low living standards is confirmed again by evidence on the availability of physicians and dentists per 100,000. The existing information spans 122 countries. These estimates are rather tricky, since the quality of doctors varies from one country to another and there are also different systems of medicine. An Indian patient has access to modern doctors, as well as to indigenous physicians practising the ancient Hindu methods and the medieval Moslem art of healing. The Chinese communes run modern and traditional practices in harness. In large areas of Africa, the tribal witch-doctors still practise their craft. The international comparisons attempted here do not effectively meet these objections. They are, however, adequate to support the general observation that underdeveloped countries tend to have below-average medical facilities. Among the listed countries, for instance, eighty-seven have availability estimates below the world mean; and these are overwhelmingly underdeveloped countries (see figure 6). A thick belt of countries in which the availability of medical practitioners is low spreads across the continents of Latin America, Africa and Asia, contrasting with the impressive availability enjoyed by Australia, the Soviet Union and higher per capita income countries of North America and Western Europe.

The incidence of literacy among different countries also conforms to the general pattern observed so far. Indeed, distribution of countries according to percentages of literate adults reveals a highly unsatisfactory performance on the part of underdeveloped countries. The relevant information is available for 136 countries for 1950 (see figure 7). International comparability is not always smooth: the *level* of literacy may vary significantly between countries. These qualifications apart, low rates of literacy characterise substantial areas in Latin America, Africa, the Near East and Eastern Asia, while higher rates are to be found largely in North America, Western Europe, Communist Europe and Australia.

The impression that underdeveloped areas tend to have a lower standard of living is thus confirmed by the available evidence.

3 An international issue

Affluence thus contrasts sharply with intolerably low income levels in a shrinking world. Inadequate medical facilities and illiteracy in many underdeveloped areas are set against the comfortable living standards of the advanced countries.

These disparities may be growing. In several Asian countries a rapid growth of large populations drags heavily on their moderate expansion of income. On the other hand, with the impressive exceptions of the Soviet Union and West Germany (matched only by Japan), the majority of the advanced countries have witnessed average rates of growth in the postwar period of only between 2% and 5%. The contrast in incomes between rich and poor nations thus may not have increased. In fact, some recent statistical investigations suggest that it has not. However, whether or not the gap is widening, the present contrast is so striking and the minimum incomes are so low that only an extraordinary insensitivity could insulate one from deep concern.

National necessity

The need for a higher growth rate in the underdeveloped areas has become inescapable. The imagination of many of these nations has been fired, perhaps most of all, by the remarkable way in which the Soviet Union has raised itself to the status of a Great Power by its own bootstraps and in a short span of time. The expansion is also demanded by the ex-colonial status of many of these countries: assertions of equal status with the erstwhile rulers ring hollow unless they are matched by economic strength. Several nationalist governments have also come to power on the promise of progress, nourished over numerous years on the thesis that foreign rule denied prosperity. Democratic forms of government, left as a legacy to some of these areas, also make the system vulnerable to insufficient growth and hence keep it alive to the issue. Even dictatorships have sometimes shown themselves sensitive to the perils implicit in an unsatisfactory rate of growth. However, in far too many instances, entrenched interests continue to stand myopically in the way of the measures that growth demands, but which require the surrender of traditional privilege and power.

International concern

The question of the growth of underdeveloped nations has simultaneously moved closer to the centre of the international scene for a combination of political and humanitarian reasons.

The political tensions implicit in the inadequate progress of two-thirds of the world's population have become increasingly clear. The difficulties of peaceful co-existence between nations that are poles apart on the income-scale are appreciated even by those who reject the Marxist categories of social and historical analysis.

These tensions are reinforced by the fact that, by historical accident, the underdeveloped nations happen to be overwhelmingly non-white. The biased allocation of world affluence to the white race lends an ugly and dangerous accent to a situation that is explosive enough in itself. Add to this the imperialist associations of the richer nations and the stage is set for a near-catastrophe.

The influx of the poorer nations into international organisations, and the sheer weight of their numbers, have relentlessly brought the problems of development to the agenda of world deliberations.

In its shift to the field of economic aid and assistance to the neutral countries since Soviet de-Stalinisation, the cold war has also taken a socially more advantageous form which assists the cause of development.

The entire process has been further accelerated by the tireless efforts of social scientists who have done much, through popular writings, to arouse world conscience on the issue. The most imaginative and radical of these writers conceive the question as one of adapting to the international framework the ethical premise of egalitarianism now accepted by most Western societies within their own national frontiers. The issue, to them, is humanitarian and essentially moral: assistance from the rich to the poor nations ought to be an ethical necessity, a compulsive moral tenet. How-

Table 2. *Industrial distribution of gross domestic product, by country, average for 1950–1 and 1958–9.* The thirteen underdeveloped countries are those listed individually. The high-income countries are Belgium, Canada, Denmark, West Germany, France, Netherlands, Norway, U.K. and U.S.A. The figures in the last three lines are simple, country averages. There are some variations in dates and classifications between countries.

Country or group	Commodity production and basic facilities						Services
	Total	Manufacturing	Industry Basic facilities	Construction	Primary production (agriculture and mining)	Total	
Ceylon	20	5	6	9	51	71	29
Tanganyika	19	7	7	6	64	84	16
Indonesia	–	9	–	–	59	–	–
Korea (Rep.)	17	9	4	4	42	59	41
Kenya	22	9	9	4	44	66	33
United Arab Republic	–	10	–	3	38	51	49
Pakistan	–	10	3	–	57	70	30
Burma	16	11	2	3	46	62	38
Congo (Leopoldville)	25	12	8	5	46	72	28
Thailand	19	13	4	2	50	69	31
India	17	17	–	–	50	67	33
Peru	26	16	7	3	36	62	38
Taiwan	30	18	7	5	34	64	36
Thirteen Underdeveloped Countries	19	11	5	4	47	67	33
Thirty-five Underdeveloped Countries	26	15	6	5	32	–	42
High-income countries	49	32	11	6	13	63	37

The problem of developing the underdeveloped world has become an urgent international issue. *Right:* construction work proceeding at Binza under a massive public works programme launched by the Congolese government, as part of the U.N. civil operations and technical assistance programme. *Below:* a group of young farmers in Taiwan receiving instruction before setting out on an agricultural mission to Liberia.

ever much this notion contrasts with political realities, it has given the liberal imagination a fresh lease of life.

The focus on problems of development has shown itself in various ways. More and more governments in underdeveloped countries have begun to commit themselves to economic progress by the formulation of Plans. By 1960, several countries – among them Ceylon, Pakistan, the U.A.R., India and China – had multi-year programmes. The growth of aid and assistance to these countries, no matter how sporadic and *ad hoc*, is also impressive. In the decade 1950–60, over $15 billion flowed to the under-developed world. This sum, less than 0·1 % of the national income of the affluent nations, is hardly satisfactory; yet it represents a significant trend.

In declaring the 1960's U.N. Decade of Development the United Nations General Assembly has, with great insight, captured one of the most prominent moods of recent years. The overall aim is to improve the preceding decade's 3 % annual rate of income

growth for the underdeveloped economies by an additional 2%. More recently, the U.N. Conference on Trade and Development has committed the international community to tackle the international economic problems arising from rapid development.

Difficulties ahead

While the challenge of development has been recognised and formally accepted, the tasks it imposes are immense. History shows not only that rapid economic progress is possible but also, indeed more emphatically, how costly and complex it is, even in the most favourable circumstances. Besides, many of the currently underdeveloped countries are starting out with a deadweight of political and sociological handicaps which some of the countries that expanded rapidly in the last century do not appear to have had.

For instance, countries such as Mauritius, China and India are under heavy population pressure, aggravated by a large base and a rising net reproduction rate, in contrast to the United States and Australia in the nineteenth century. Political difficulties also beset many nations in a manner that carries heavy economic cost. Border disputes, for example, necessitate military expenditures in India, Pakistan and Malaysia; racial tension disrupts stability in British Guiana and Indonesia; feudal kingdoms in the Middle East have a weakness for spending scarce resources on lavish consumption; military dictatorships stage coups in Latin America, preventing genuine progress from taking root.

Cultural traditions are frequently incompatible with the pursuit of material improvement. Religious beliefs permit aged cattle to subsist on scarce food and agile monkeys to ravage standing crops in the Indian state of United Provinces.

The external economic environment has also become generally difficult. Flows of private capital, large-scale immigrations which brought in unskilled as well as skilled labour and the burgeoning trade which sparked off some remarkable industrialisations in the nineteenth century have no counterpart in the modern world.

At the same time, better communications have collapsed most nations into a close-knit network, adding in some ways to the difficulties of mobilisation for development in many poorer countries. Awareness that higher living standards exist, while generating development-consciousness, also makes these standards more difficult to attain: everyone demands higher standards immediately, whereas growth requires savings which entail restraint in the present. In this matter the role of many international agencies has also been two-sided. The International Labour Organisation, for instance, works with notions of labour welfare which are far too expensive for most developing countries.

The process of transformation is inevitably complex. Difficulties exist at several levels, defining the constraints within which the targets of income expansion have to be implemented. The economic and social structures of the underdeveloped countries are of central significance in this respect. They have to be understood before the problems of growth can be handled.

PART TWO

The economic and social structure

An Ifugao tribesman looks out over the Banawe rice-terraces, in Luzon Province in the Philippines. Agriculture in most underdeveloped countries is handicapped by primitive techniques and lack of innovation, but these terraces offer an interesting exception. They date back some 4,000 years and still rank as a remarkable feat of water-engineering.

4 Production and occupational structure

Generalisations in the social sciences have now become suspect. Social anthropologists are among the most prominent converts to this mood of scepticism: they have moved perceptibly from searching for laws of universal validity to intensive analysis of the structure of specific societies. Even when stable relationships are observed, few can be regarded as significant.

Indeed, economic and social characteristics vary between different underdeveloped countries. Explosive rates of population growth, instability of export earnings and religious attitudes inhibiting development, for example, are unevenly distributed among the poor nations. Nevertheless, there are many economic and social aspects which are both significant and relevant to fairly large numbers of underdeveloped countries. And these certainly need to be analysed and assessed.

Production structure

Economists generally classify economic activity into three groups: 1 industrial, 2 primary and 3 tertiary. The first group includes manufacturing, extending to construction and 'basic facilities' such as electricity undertakings. The second group relates to agricultural activity and mining, and the third to commerce, trade and services. Such classifications are interesting only in so far as they lead to conclusions of significance. In this instance, at least two notable propositions emerge from the available data on production structure.

On the one hand, the underdeveloped countries seem to have, on the average, a lower proportion of industrial output than the higher-income countries. On the other hand, the share of the tertiary sector in total output does not appear to be significantly lower in the underdeveloped countries (as seen in table 2). The conclusion to be drawn from these two observations is that the share of the primary sector in the underdeveloped areas is significantly larger, on the average, than in the group of advanced countries. If the data are reclassified so as to put mining into the industrial sector, and agricultural activity alone is classified as

Figure 8. *Percentage of active population in agricultural occupations and underdevelopment, several dates mostly in 1940's and 1950's.* Percentage of active population in agricultural occupations which are *above* the world mean (calculated from the available statistics of 97 countries) are found exclusively

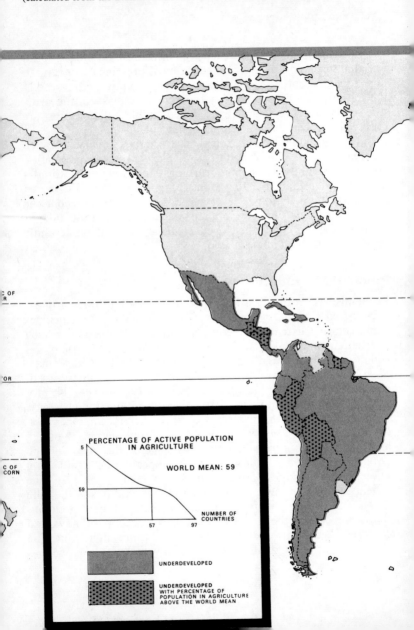

PERCENTAGE OF ACTIVE POPULATION
IN AGRICULTURE

WORLD MEAN: 59

5

59

57   97

NUMBER OF
COUNTRIES

UNDERDEVELOPED

UNDERDEVELOPED
WITH PERCENTAGE OF
POPULATION IN AGRICULTURE
ABOVE THE WORLD MEAN

in the underdeveloped countries. Further, several underdeveloped countries have larger percentages of agricultural population than most advanced countries. There are, however, some prominent exceptions: the Soviet Union has 50% (1950) whereas Argentina has only 25% (1947) and Chile 30% (1952).

primary, the conclusion still holds. There are exceptions. Some advanced countries have fairly high proportions of primary activity: Denmark, New Zealand, Belgium and the Netherlands are noted for their high levels of agricultural production. But this does not controvert the stated propositions which relate to *average* characteristics. It does, however, help to underline the fallacy implicit in deducing, directly from these propositions, the necessity to industrialise if higher per capita incomes are desired.

Occupational structure

The concentration of underdeveloped countries on primary, and especially agricultural, output is matched by a similar concentration of the working force in this sector (see figure 8). But more significant is the fact that the latter concentration appears to be impressively larger. In documenting and drawing inferences from this contrast, it is necessary to appreciate some of the principal limitations of occupational data.

Occupational distribution figures are difficult to compile. Moreover, it is hazardous to compare them between countries. Much of the difficulty springs from the fact that people tend to have more than one occupation. How is the statistician to classify the Kenyan who works in the urban factory but continues to return to his *samba* for his ploughing and harvesting seasons? Moneylenders who are also traders and cultivators are a common phenomenon in parts of India. This multiplicity of roles in the economic sphere cuts across neatly separated occupational categories. It is perhaps most relevant to the underdeveloped countries where specialisation in economic roles may not have developed. Inevitably, conventions have to be adopted to handle these problems. For instance, a labourer who derives more than half his income from an occupation may be classified as belonging to it. These conventions differ between countries, and, indeed, between different censuses and enquiries in the same country; thus, it is often difficult to secure the necessary standard of comparison.

None the less, conclusions can be drawn since it is possible to assess the magnitude of these difficulties and to infer the direction in which adjustments need to be made in the available data. It is clear, for instance, that the number in agricultural occupations is somewhat exaggerated, while those in the tertiary sector are understated: a fraction of the working force in the former is partially engaged in the latter. But while any correction would certainly shift the relative numbers in favour of the tertiary group, firsthand observation and detailed analysis rule out any major change.

Making allowances for complications in this fashion, it is still possible to maintain that the underdeveloped countries have, generally speaking, a higher proportion of their working force in agriculture and a lower proportion in industrial activity than the high-income countries (see figures 8–10). There are a few exceptions to these generalisations: the Soviet Union, for example, has nearly half its working force in agriculture.

Another significant proposition that survives scrutiny concerns the contrast that exists in many cases between the proportion of primary to total production and the share of the working force engaged in primary occupations. Many agriculture-based, advanced countries, such as Denmark, Belgium and Australia have high agricultural activity but a small agricultural working force. By contrast, several underdeveloped countries (e.g. China and India) have a strikingly greater proportion of agricultural employment than output. This means that, in these countries, productivity in agriculture is less than in other occupations.

Surplus labour

This phenomenon of low productivity can be explained in terms of the 'underemployment' of much agricultural labour in these countries. The pressure of population, combined with the fact that few non-agricultural jobs are available, may have led to more and more people being absorbed on the land itself. The institution of the

Figure 9. *Percentage of labour force in secondary production, several dates.* Underdeveloped countries generally have a lower proportion of their labour force in secondary production (which includes manufacturing and, as a rule, mining and construction).

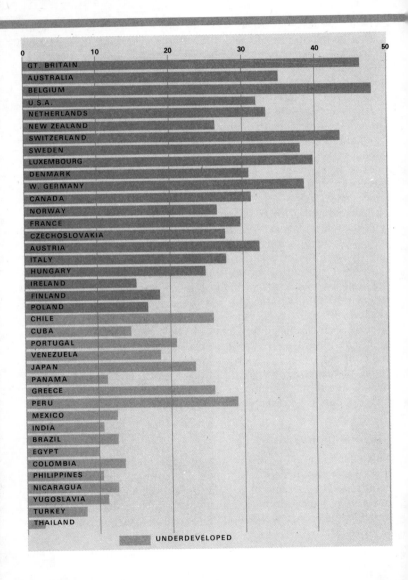

Figure 10. *Percentage of labour force engaged in tertiary production, several dates mostly in 1940's, set against income per capita in United States dollars, about 1949.* Underdeveloped countries seem generally to have a lower proportion of their labour force engaged in tertiary production (which includes commerce, trade, transport and communications, government and other services). These data, however, offer serious difficulties of interpretation (see text).

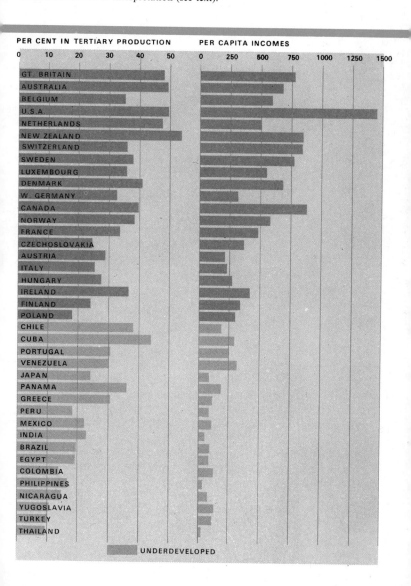

PER CENT IN TERTIARY PRODUCTION   PER CAPITA INCOMES

GT. BRITAIN
AUSTRALIA
BELGIUM
U.S.A.
NETHERLANDS
NEW ZEALAND
SWITZERLAND
SWEDEN
LUXEMBOURG
DENMARK
W. GERMANY
CANADA
NORWAY
FRANCE
CZECHOSLOVAKIA
AUSTRIA
ITALY
HUNGARY
IRELAND
FINLAND
POLAND
CHILE
CUBA
PORTUGAL
VENEZUELA
JAPAN
PANAMA
GREECE
PERU
MEXICO
INDIA
BRAZIL
EGYPT
COLOMBIA
PHILIPPINES
NICARAGUA
YUGOSLAVIA
TURKEY
THAILAND

UNDERDEVELOPED

A primitive donkey-powered well near Doha, Qatar.

extended peasant family is likely to have facilitated this process: the growing numbers would be supported as dependants with an effective claim on the income while the limited work on the family farm would be 'shared' with them. The sharing-out of the work would necessarily be accompanied by the creation of underemployment.

Reflecting on this phenomenon, economists have characterised the resulting situation as one of 'disguised unemployment'. If fulltime 'normal' work were done by only a fraction of the total number who share the farming chores, the farm output would be as high as before and the rest of the 'workers' would be shown up as redundant, 'surplus' – in fact unemployed.

In practice, it has been found very difficult to assess the significance of this phenomenon. How many hours of work must be regarded as 'normal' in the calculation? Since organisational and technological changes can always improve productivity in an activity, thereby displacing some employed labour, these must be ruled out: the computation must assume that no such improvements are implemented. But then impossible difficulties arise. Sociologists have noted that underemployment has frequently been interwoven, over time, into the social fabric. If some workers *were* in fact taken off the farm, a few social and economic changes would become inevitable. These would surely classify as organisational changes. Economists have further found, for instance, that much of the redundant labour manages to keep itself reasonably employed at the harvesting season. Any removal of this labour, therefore, would necessitate organisational changes to bring in the harvest.

But quite apart from such conceptual difficulties involved in measuring the degree of underemployment, one cannot deny the presence of the phenomenon and its immediate impact on the productivity of labour in the agriculture of some populous underdeveloped countries.

Primitive techniques and self-subsistence

Labour productivity, however, is inadequate in *all* economic activity in most underdeveloped countries. This naturally reflects the low per capita incomes in these areas. But there is a little more to it than that. In many cases, the techniques in use are *primitive*. The scientific revolution has bypassed whole segments of these economies. Inadequacy of knowledge and unwillingness to innovate are among the principal factors that account for this backwardness.

These are incontrovertible facts, though it is possible to exaggerate them. Striking examples of human ingenuity can be found in the least likely places. The rice-terraces carved out centuries ago on the steep slopes of the Luzon mountains in the Philippines by Ifugao

tribesmen are still among the more impressive innovations in agriculture. The most fruitful advances in technical knowledge in the post-Meiji agricultural revolution in Japan during the late nineteenth century came from adaptations of the farming practices observed on the land itself. Moreover, the willingness to innovate is evident in the introduction of new crops (e.g. the potato in India) and the conversion of farming lands in order to increase production of profitable cash crops (e.g. cocoa in West Africa). However, despite these qualifications, the level and the rate of change of techniques in the underdeveloped areas are woefully inadequate.

They are associated further with a relatively less pronounced reliance on the market mechanism than in the economies of the advanced countries. The role of self-subsistence is greater. Many households produce for themselves and engage in limited exchange. Moreover, much of this exchange takes the form of 'barter' – i.e. commodities are exchanged directly, instead of through the medium of money. This barter sometimes dovetails into social institutions: the barber and the washerman in many Indian villages exchange their services for stated bushels of grain from higher-caste peasant families. Ritual 'payments', in goods, to brahmins, headmen, witch-doctors and others for their services are a widespread phenomenon, well-documented by anthropologists.

The market *does* exist, of course, in practically all societies. Markets cater to both barter and 'monetised' exchange. The former can be found in many African and Asian countries. The latter are almost as common: the Malay fishermen, for instance, sell to merchants on the seashore and the fish is carried into the larger markets of the hinterland by water. Indeed, monetised markets date back for centuries: Indian and Arab merchants were engaged in remunerative trade, spanning continents, as early as the Middle Ages. But even today, the role of exchange is relatively limited in underdeveloped areas; and monetised exchange is even more so.

Cocoa bags being unloaded from railway vans at Takoradi harbour, Ghana. Cocoa provides over 60% of Ghana's total export earnings. It is often said that countries which rely on few export commodities, as most underdeveloped countries do, are subject to greater instability. But fluctuations in export earnings are no greater than for the advanced countries.

5 Links with the international economy

The way the underdeveloped countries are integrated into the international economy, is as important as their internal economic and social structure. This is widely appreciated. Indeed, a large number of hypotheses concerning the international aspects of underdeveloped countries can be found in the popular literature.

It is claimed, for instance, that they suffer from an adverse, long-term decline in the terms at which they exchange their exports for imports; that their export earnings are subject to an acute instability, more pronounced than in the advanced countries; that their export prospects are not bright; that private capital does not flow to them any longer in adequate quantities. Many of these theses have strong emotional and political overtones. Facts, therefore, tend to get distorted and arguments frequently turn into assertions. Yet there is often a great deal of truth embedded in some of these generalisations. It is worth sorting out the issues clearly and sifting the evidence to examine how much survives careful analysis.

Adverse secular trend in the terms of trade

Several analysts, including international organisations, have lent support to the view that the terms at which underdeveloped countries exchange their products for imports have been registering a secular (i.e. long-term) decline. It has been claimed, for instance, that between the latter part of the last century and 1939, there was a fall in the prices of primary goods relative to the prices of manufactures. On the average, a given bundle of primary goods reduced, in exchange, to 60% of the quantity of manufactures that could be secured earlier. From this, it has been deduced that there must have been a comparable worsening of the terms of trade of the underdeveloped countries.

It is easy to see what is wrong with this argument. 1 It is not possible to infer the behaviour of the terms of trade of under-developed countries directly from that of primary products *vis-à-vis* manufactures. The underdeveloped countries export

Figure 11. *Percentage of foreign exchange earnings from three principal export commodities for 62 countries, 1957.* Several underdeveloped countries derive strikingly high proportions of their foreign exchange earnings from a few export commodities.

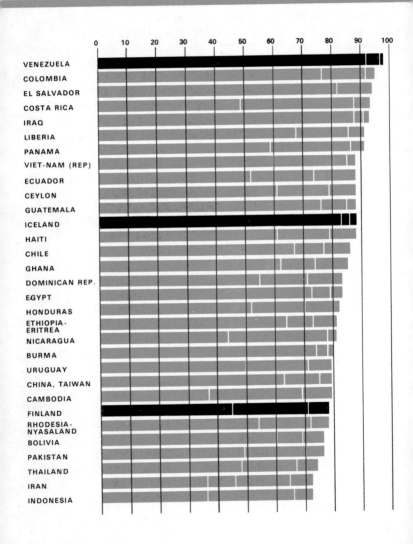

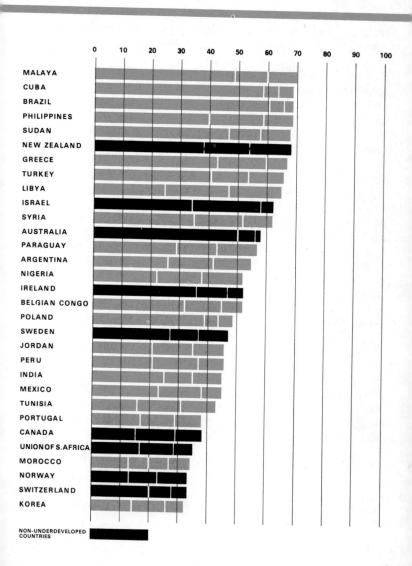

	0	10	20	30	40	50	60	70	80	90	100
MALAYA											
CUBA											
BRAZIL											
PHILIPPINES											
SUDAN											
NEW ZEALAND											
GREECE											
TURKEY											
LIBYA											
ISRAEL											
SYRIA											
AUSTRALIA											
PARAGUAY											
ARGENTINA											
NIGERIA											
IRELAND											
BELGIAN CONGO											
POLAND											
SWEDEN											
JORDAN											
PERU											
INDIA											
MEXICO											
TUNISIA											
PORTUGAL											
CANADA											
UNION OF S. AFRICA											
MOROCCO											
NORWAY											
SWITZERLAND											
KOREA											
NON-UNDERDEVELOPED COUNTRIES											

different types of primary products and sometimes even manufactures; they also import different types of manufactures and sometimes even primary products. Any aggregated analysis of primary products v. manufactures will, therefore, *not* give a firm clue to the behaviour of the terms of trade of underdeveloped countries. Indeed, only very few countries have yet been studied and the results are not always consistent with the thesis of a secular adverse trend. 2 The index as computed tends to understate the gains of primary exporters in trade. Manufactures have improved tremendously in quality over the period, but the index hardly allows for this. 3 Finally, the index refers to the British data for the period. This again overstates the loss of the primary producers, as transport costs were falling over the period. Since British prices are used, the primary product prices include transport costs and hence fall due to transport cost reduction, whereas the manufactures prices exclude transport costs and do not register a corresponding fall. If, instead, the prices were computed from the viewpoint of the primary producing, underdeveloped countries, the resulting index would show a far smaller decline in the terms of trade of underdeveloped countries.

Perhaps the firmest conclusion that can be sustained by the economist is that, at the moment, it is impossible to derive any convincing proposition either way concerning the *past* behaviour of the terms of trade of the underdeveloped countries as a group except for short periods such as 1950–62 when the terms of trade did deteriorate for them.

The question of the *future* trend is also intractable. Several, very different, projections are currently available. For every projection which contains a gloomy prospect for the underdeveloped countries, there is a matching forecast of improvement!

Concentration and instability of export earnings

There is also a widespread belief that the underdeveloped countries rely too heavily on export earnings from a few primary commodities, suffering consequently from sharp instability in the

Sudanese women picking cotton,
their country's chief source
of export earnings.

59

capacity to import their requirements. This thesis has weaknesses very similar to those affecting the question of the adverse secular behaviour of the terms of trade.

Export earnings of the underdeveloped countries are certainly concentrated in several instances (see figure 11). Ninety-five per cent of Colombia's earnings come from coffee, petroleum and bananas; 88% of Ceylon's from tea, rubber and coconut products. More than twenty underdeveloped countries rely on just one commodity for more than 50% of their earnings. Striking examples are provided by the earnings of Ecuador from bananas (52%), Cuba from sugar (59%), Ghana from cacao (62%), Egypt from cotton (72%) and Burma from rice (74%). There is *no* evidence however of a significant inverse relationship between per capita income and concentration of earnings on a few export commodities (see figure 12).

While the evidence underscores the presence of *concentration*, it does not bear out the hypotheses about *instability* of export earnings. The export earnings of the underdeveloped countries

Figure 12. *G.N.P. per capita related to the proportion of export earnings coming from three principal export commodities*. No significant relation between these two variables emerges from the available statistics. A lower per capita income thus does not seem to be generally associated with greater concentration. This is consistent with the fact that many low-income countries have significant concentration of export earnings on a few export commodities.

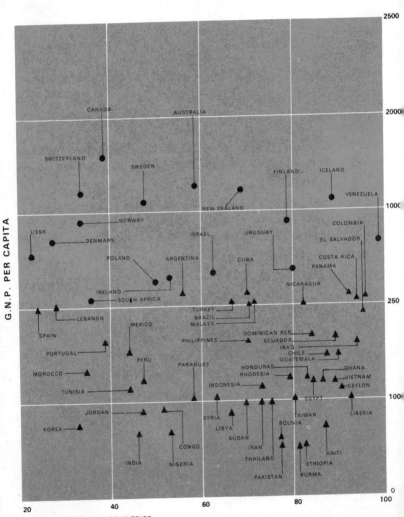

certainly fluctuate, but it cannot be maintained that these fluctuations are larger than those in the high-income countries. Nor is it possible to claim that there is any significant link between instability and per capita income (see figure 13). Instability is *not* greater when per capita incomes are lower. The instability of Austrian, Finnish, French and Australian export earnings, for instance, has recently been greater than that for Turkey, the (former) Belgian Congo, El Salvador, Spain, Guatemala and Ceylon.

A significant link between concentration and instability is therefore improbable. Indeed, this is what the evidence suggests. This refutation of the popular association of concentration with instability continues even when the concentration is interpreted with respect to 1 earnings from one commodity or 2 undue reliance on certain markets (i.e. *regional* concentration). Neither of these indices shows a significant relationship with the instability of export earnings.

Two principal conclusions alone survive scrutiny for most underdeveloped countries: 1 instability in export earnings is fairly high; and 2 these earnings come largely from a few primary commodities. These propositions are modest; but they are significant. Instability poses problems of domestic and international adjustment which few economic administrations in the underdeveloped countries are either trained or equipped to solve. A nation that concentrates on a limited range of primary exports faces the risk that the markets for them may have limited prospects of expansion. Indeed, this problem has won more and more attention in view of the need for expanding export earnings to finance the import requirements of developmental plans.

Prospects for export expansion

Measured in terms of the rate at which their export earnings have been expanding, the performance of the underdeveloped areas has been disappointing. Their share in the value of world exports has

Table 3. *Percentage share of non-industrial countries in value of world exports.* All Soviet-area exports have been omitted. The non-industrial group also includes Australia and New Zealand and excludes Japan. With these qualifications, which do not alter the true picture, the data can be taken to indicate the direction and magnitude of change in the export share of the underdeveloped countries.

	Including oil-exporting countries		Excluding oil-exporting countries	
	1928	1957	1928	1957
Share in world exports	33·8	31·3	32·2	24·4

fallen in the thirty years since 1928; and the fall is significant when the few fortunate oil-producers are excluded from the picture (see table 3). This share has fallen at a time when the average rate of growth of world trade has been *lower* than in the nineteenth century. The unimpressive export performance of the under-developed countries, both in itself and relative to the advanced countries, has led economists to speculate about its causes.

The 'export lag' has been attributed to the gradual deceleration in the demand for primary products which constitute, as already noted, the bulk of the exports from the underdeveloped nations. Several factors have converged fortuitously to lead to this decelera-tion. Many countries have suffered from the displacement of primary products by synthetic substitutes, relentlessly pursued in this Age of the Chemical Revolution. Chicle is no longer necessary to chewing gum; synthetic rubber has taken over many of the uses of natural rubber; nylon fibres have steadily intruded into the markets for finer textiles; steel is giving way more and more to titanium, magnesium and the new, harder plastics. Some markets have also been ruined by changes in organisational methods: jute bags have no function when bulk-handling methods are adopted or when paper packages are preferred for their capacity to take the attractive designs and prints which motivate purchases in super-markets. Again, in many areas, scientific inventions have reduced the use of raw materials per unit output: automation, for instance, has cut down wastage in textiles. Greater efficiency in the recovery of materials has helped the process: scrap iron is a good example.

Figure 13. *G.N.P. per capita related to the index of instability in export earnings.* A significant relation does not appear to emerge from the available data. This is consistent, however, with the presence of considerable instability in export earnings in many underdeveloped countries.

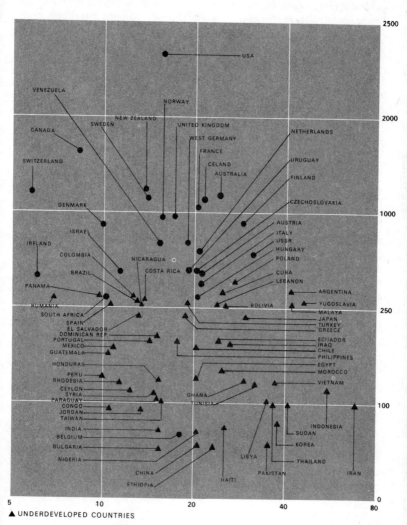

EXPORT INSTABILITY INDEX

▲ UNDERDEVELOPED COUNTRIES

Of course, not everything can be explained in these terms. Some countries have certainly followed domestic policies which have led to poor export performance even though foreign markets were favourable: Argentina, under Peron, fits this thesis admirably. Sometimes markets have been permanently lost as a result of artificial scarcities caused originally by calamities such as war: the substitution of paper for jute in packing began seriously during the Second World War. Sometimes the cause may have been the exhaustion of supplies, as with minerals. However, these supply factors represent relatively trivial instances. The bulk of the explanation seems to be provided by the influences that operate on the *demand* for the primary exports of the underdeveloped countries.

While this analysis underlines the relatively dim prospects for expansion of earnings by underdeveloped countries *as a group*, it is not the same as arguing that *each* underdeveloped country has bad prospects. Different countries export different primary products; and even where they export the same commodities, the share of each commodity in the total exports will be different. Add to this diversity the fact that there are significant variations in the prospects of expansion of different commodities and it is easy to see that *some* underdeveloped countries may be in a less uncomfortable situation (closer to that of the oil-producers). Again, a shift towards greater reliance on the exports of manufactures provides some countries with an escape valve. Even here, however, the situation is complicated by the fact that the developed countries use import quotas and tariffs against 'cheap-labour' products from the poor nations, and by the stiff competition which is offered in many markets by established producers from the advanced countries.

The international flow of capital

As with the growth of exports, the twentieth-century experience of underdeveloped countries with respect to the inflow of private capital has been disappointing when measured by the yardstick of

Figure 14. *Percentage distribution of net bilateral flow of long-term capital (including official donations) from developed, private enterprise economies (excluding communist countries) to underdeveloped countries, by source, average for 1960–1.* The United States is dominant, with France following.

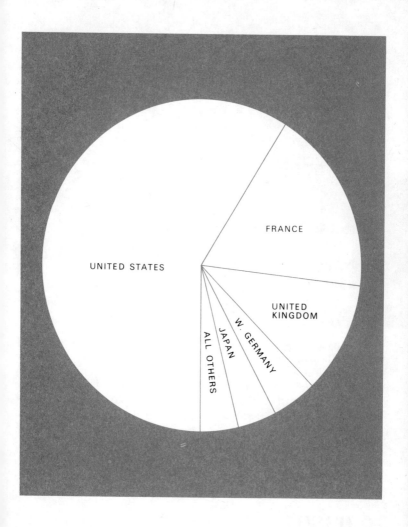

the preceding century. Capital is indeed moving from the advanced
to the underdeveloped countries. In 1956 alone, $5 billion flowed
in this direction. By 1960–1, this sum had exceeded $7 billion.
As a proportion of world trade, this does not compare unfavourably with previous experience.

The differences arise in the composition of this flow. More than
half of it consists now of official transfers. The flow of *private*
capital by itself has definitely ebbed. The reasons are not difficult to
seek and are largely tied up with those underlying the lag in exports
from the underdeveloped countries. Much of the nineteenth-century

Looking for oil in Libya.
Few underdeveloped countries
are in the lucky position
of the oil-producers.

67

flow of capital was used to exploit the natural resources which constituted the exports to the advanced countries. Growing export markets for the developing countries thus also meant a growing inflow of capital into them from the developed nations. This nexus still persists by and large; but now it implies low flows of private capital because of the reduced profitability of many of the primary markets. The flow of private capital has been sustained at its current level largely by the continued attractiveness of a few primary products (e.g. the oil producers have had no difficulty in finding foreign capital) and partly by the sporadic profitability of some domestic industries in these regions (e.g. Swedish investment in the paper industry in India). There is some prospect that the latter factor will grow in importance with the formulation of developmental plans in underdeveloped regions.

Three further aspects of the international flow of capital are worth noting. 1 The share of official *donations* has increased in the last decade. 2 The centrally-planned communist economies have emerged as an important source of long-term credit and occasionally of grants. Among the 'capitalist' countries, the United States continues to remain the largest source of capital and donations, with France and the U.K. leading the rest (see figure 14). Among the communist countries, the Soviet Union dominates the scene, followed by Czechoslovakia (see figure 15). 3 Finally, there has also been a steady expansion in the activity of multilateral lending agencies which extend long-term loans. Prominent among these is the World Bank.

This, then, is the external environment facing the underdeveloped countries. As members of the international economy, these countries appear to be vulnerable in three ways: 1 their export earnings are unstable; 2 the prospects for expanding these earnings are not very bright; and 3 inflows of private capital from the advanced countries are not substantial and underline the strategic role of foreign aid in filling the gap. These are precisely the areas where the developed countries can assist in adjusting the international economy.

Figure 15. *Centrally planned economies: commitments of bilateral economic assistance to underdeveloped countries, by source.* In terms of *commitment of assistance*, as also of actual expenditures, the Soviet Union is naturally preponderant although its role has diminished recently. Such assistance has grown in recent years, though the amount from the 'free enterprise' economies is strikingly greater.

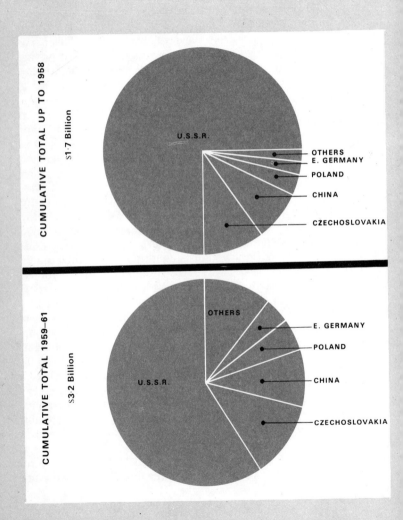

6 The paucity of savings

The role of savings in promoting development is rarely called into question. Many writers cite the paucity of savings as the principal cause of underdevelopment. They point to the link between savings and investment and, in turn, between investment and the growth of income. This chain of reasoning is substantially valid. But in spite of its apparent simplicity the argument is really so complex that it is important to grasp it well.

Savings for investment

Why do we need savings for investment? If a well has to be dug, for instance, does it necessarily imply *abstinence* on someone's part? Suppose a hundred unemployed workers are hired to work on the project. They will be paid wages. These earnings will lead to increased expenditure on consumption in so far as the hundred workers spend their incomes. As a result, the price level of consumer goods will rise *unless* 1 additional supplies materialise from somewhere or 2 someone ceases to buy consumer goods by an equivalent amount. The former possibility is realistic only in the context of foreign aid; in this case, the consumer goods will come from abroad, as indeed wheat goes from the United States to many underdeveloped countries (under the Public Law 480 programme). This implies, of course, that the foreigners forego the consumption of these commodities. The savings are then *foreign* saving. If this happy possibility is ruled out, and if price inflation is to be avoided, the expenditure on consumer goods will have to be reduced by others *domestically* so as to accommodate the increased demand of the newly hired workers. This will then be *domestic* saving.

Four other possibilities also exist: 1 The hundred workers may not spend their incomes at all. In this event, it is they who are doing the necessary saving which permits the investment in the well to be carried out. 2 They may be exhorted to 'donate' their labour without remuneration. If so, they can again be regarded as having contributed the required saving. This is actually a phenomenon of some importance. As we shall discuss later (in chapter 17), many countries with surplus labour have attempted to get labour-intensive investments (such as drainage, digging wells, levelling roads, building mud schoolhouses) carried out through voluntary, *gratis* work. These attempts have sometimes formed the core of the Community Development Programmes, directed at rural transformation. 3 A further possibility concerns the situation when *no* additional saving materialises from anywhere to match the investment in the well. In this case, prices will rise, the demand for consumer goods having risen in relation to their supply. This *inflation* of prices, however, itself signifies the emergence of the required savings. The available consumer goods are now being *shared* between the previous buyers and the hundred workers; the money incomes of the former purchase less goods (in view of the rise in prices) and the remaining commodities now accrue to the latter. This is a phenomenon aptly described as *forced savings*. And it is a method of 'financing' investments which is favoured by many governments, especially in Latin America. 4 Finally, there is another way in which the government could create the required savings. If people will not *voluntarily* forego consumption to avoid the excess demand for commodities, the authorities can impose additional *taxation* to generate the necessary abstinence forcibly. This is clearly not an easy thing for governments to undertake. And yet it is a more efficient and equitable method of financing investments than inflation.

While illustrative examples could be multiplied, the essential role of savings in creating investment is substantially contained in the analysis so far. It is necessary now to examine different forms and sources of saving and their incidence in the underdeveloped countries.

Different types of saving

It will already have become apparent that savings can come from foreign or from domestic sources. Foreign savings can accrue to a country in varying forms. Private investments and aid of varying types are typical examples. How is the magnitude of foreign savings accruing to a country to be measured? The answer is simple and rests on an elementary proposition: in so far as there is any excess of import expenditure over export earnings, the country is getting *more* resources from abroad than it gives in exchange. This excess measures the precise extent to which foreigners abstain from using their resources for themselves and make these 'saved' resources available for the other country's use. These resources may have to be returned later – as, for instance, when foreign aid has to be repaid. But at the time these foreign resources (appropriately described by economists as foreign savings) add to the total resources available for use.

The proportion of these foreign savings to domestic savings at any moment differs widely from one country to another. In South Korea recently, the volume of foreign savings has been very high owing to United States military expenditure, whereas domestic savings have sometimes even been nil! On the other hand, the Soviet Union has developed with a more or less insignificant inflow of foreign savings and with significant increases in domestic savings.

Domestic savings similarly come from different sources. *Individuals* can save. The savings of individuals (or households) are the difference between their income and their current expenditure. *Corporations* can also save. In so far as they do not distribute their entire profits, they save. *Local and central governments* are in a position to save as well. They earn income from investments, taxes and levies; and they spend on various items of current expenditure (such as wages and salaries of employees). The difference constitutes their savings.

Statistics on the size and composition of savings in underdeveloped countries are hard to come by. Even countries with advanced statistical expertise, such as India, have begun only recently to produce the necessary estimates; and these again are not very reliable. But rough orders of magnitude are sufficient for our purpose. It is possible to infer that the proportionate contribution

Table 4. Saving by major groups for certain countries, 1955–9
(percentage of national total)

	Total	Total government	National government	State and local government	Government enterprises	Corporate	Households
Ceylon							
1955	100·0	50·8	55·5	−3·9	−0·9	6·7	42·5
1959	100·0	7·8	7·8	–	–	18·3	73·9
1955–9	100·0	38·4	47·4	–	–	13·8	47·8
Japan							
1955	100·0	19·9	–	–	–	28·3	51·8
1958	100·0	21·3	–	–	–	28·3	50·4
1955–8	100·0	21·6	–	–	–	28·8	49·5
Philippines							
1955	100·0	17·0	11·5	3·3	2·2	29·8	53·2
1959	100·0	11·0	8·7	1·2	1·0	31·7	57·3
1955–9	100·0	12·3	8·7	2·0	1·6	30·9	56·8
South Korea							
1958	100·0	−83·3	–	–	–	48·0	135·3
1959	100·0	−36·0	–	–	–	22·0	114·0
India							
1954–5	100·0	5·6	8·6	−3·0	−0·03	7·2	87·2
1957–8	100·0	13·2	10·2	2·4	0·5	2·1	84·7

made by diverse forms of domestic saving varies between countries. For instance, the contribution of the government sector in the few instances listed in table 4 ranges from nearly 50% to a dissaving of over 80%! These variations reflect differences in economic organisation and behaviour.

None the less, a few systematic relationships between backwardness and the performance of different saver-groups can be observed. The most important concerns the saving of *households*. Underdeveloped countries lean relatively heavily on households and relatively less on other saver-groups. By contrast, in many high-income countries, household savings play a significantly smaller role. This reflects again the relative growth of the corporate and governmental sectors in the advanced countries.

Pattern of household savings and its implications

Household savings are held in varying forms. Gold happens to be favoured in many underdeveloped countries. There is also a noticeable preference in these countries for 'tangible' as against 'financial' assets (see figure 16). Instead of holding deposits with banks, shares and other financial investments, households hold their savings in physical form: bullocks, residential property, grain, farm improvements and so on. Both these patterns of saving-behaviour have an economic rationale. Gold is preferred as a hedge against inflation. Moreover, tangible assets are held in the absence of banks and other institutions necessary for the creation of financial assets. Finally, a large part of the household saving is 'non-monetised' and hence inevitably in physical form; bunds are built, drains are repaired, walls are plastered with cowdung and wells are dug with family labour, creating investment and constituting equivalent household savings *without* entering the market at any stage!

Because of the lack of sufficient banking and financial institutions (such as an efficient capital market), the *transfer* of funds from those who save to those who wish to invest is rarely smooth and

sometimes impossible. In many underdeveloped countries this provides a major brake on the ability to invest. What is more, in so far as banks increase willingness to save by ensuring the payment of interest on relatively safe financial investments, without such institutions household savings are jeopardised and their growth is limited.

Moreover, it is interesting to note that the tendency to use savings to purchase tangible assets such as land is sometimes socially *unproductive*. In countries such as Ceylon and India, the preference for landholding has traditionally frustrated a good deal of saving. What one individual saves and invests in land may be dissaved by another who sells the land. From the social point of view, the net effect may therefore be zero saving. The preference for land as an asset, for prestige and other social reasons, may thus act as an instrument of dissaving and hence as a brake on the national

Starting young – schoolboys in the Congo lining up at a savings bank to invest their pocket-money. Lack of savings is generally regarded as one of the chief causes of underdevelopment.

capacity to save. Indeed, the wastefulness of land-preference is compounded in other ways. For example, the sale of land by small, distressed peasants to landowners (buying it for social reasons) may result in a less efficient use of the land itself. This phenomenon has in fact been observed in several underdeveloped countries, especially in Asia, in a form which is aptly described as 'absentee landlordism'.

There are disadvantages also in some of the other forms in which households in underdeveloped countries prefer to hold their savings. Gold holdings in particular can lead to social waste. India has recently lost valuable and scarce foreign exchange through illegal payments for smuggled gold imports. Among other corrective measures a restriction on the purchase of 24-carat gold has been imposed so as to force households away from their socially deleterious attachment to gold-holding.

Governmental savings

The most interesting aspects of governmental savings in underdeveloped countries concern the tax systems generating the revenues from which they arise. By and large, there are three easily distinguished characteristics of the tax structure of underdeveloped countries.

1 Their proportion of tax revenues to national income is generally less than in advanced countries. As a proportion of G.N.P., government revenue in Burma was 18%, in Thailand 11%, in Philippines 10% and in India 9% on the average during 1950–8. Similar proportions obtain in most Latin American and African countries: 9% in Mexico, 14% in Chile and 10% in Brazil are recent examples. This contrasts with figures ranging up to 30 or even 35% in many advanced countries.

2 Moreover, most underdeveloped countries depend heavily on *indirect* taxation (on commodities) and earn a relatively insignificant amount of revenue from *direct* taxes (on income and wealth). In 1959, Sudan, Guatemala, Haiti, Iran, Jordan and Thailand derived

less than 10% of their total revenues from direct taxes. For over twenty underdeveloped countries, the figure was less than 20%. The contrasting use of income tax in advanced and underdeveloped countries is also revealing. Assessments for income tax cover 30–40% of the *total* population in advanced countries; in most countries of Asia, Africa and Latin America the figure is in the range of 1–3%. One chief reason why underdeveloped countries rely so much on indirect taxation is that it is comparatively easier to administer. Many poor nations further derive the bulk of their revenue from customs duties, imposed conveniently at the ports of entry and exit, on imports and exports. In fact taxes on imports, exports, foreign exchange and profits from state-earned export monopolies and monopolistic distribution of imported items have provided over two-fifths of the total revenue in recent years for countries such as Iran, Thailand, Burma, Ceylon and Laos.

There are two unfortunate consequences of this dependence on indirect taxation. (a) As incomes rise, the proportion of tax revenue to income generally increases under a *progressive* direct tax. For instance, let there be two income tax payers, one earning $100 and the other $200, with tax rates at 10% for the income-bracket $50–150, 20% for $151–250 and 30% for $251–400. The revenue will then be $50 on a total income of $300 – a proportion of one-sixth. Suppose now that incomes double for each individual. The revenue will then be $160 on a total income of $600 – a proportion exceeding one-sixth. A progressive tax system, which is generally what *direct* taxes constitute, thus *builds into itself* a rising proportion of tax collection to income. On the other hand, since indirect taxes are usually levied in proportion to value of commodities, the underdeveloped countries relying on them are liable to lose this important advantage. Indeed, since empirical observation suggests that the proportion of trade to national income falls as income rises, the numerous underdeveloped countries which lean heavily on customs duties for their revenues are likely to face a secular *decline* in their revenue relative to their national incomes. (b) The other consequence is a tendency to have *fluctuating* revenue.

Figure 16. *Ratios of savings in financial to savings in tangible assets in selected, low-income countries.* These ratios are generally lower than in high-income countries. The main reasons for this are a preference for tangible (i.e. physical) assets, the fact that financial assets (such as stocks and debentures) are frequently not available and the absence of developed financial institutions (such as commercial banks).

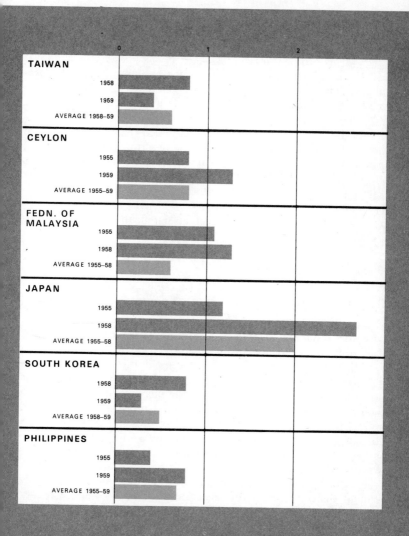

Instability in trade tends to translate itself immediately into unstable revenue, making for short-term difficulties which do not arise so readily in countries relying less on customs revenue and more on other forms of taxation.

3 Finally, in the poorer countries the agricultural sector is frequently taxed too lightly in relation to other areas of production. While farmers pay excise and sales taxes as consumers like anyone else, most of the direct taxes fall less on them, if at all. Income taxes, for instance, are usually confined to non-agricultural incomes, as in India. Land taxation (quite seriously levied in India) is fairly light in many countries – in Ghana and Turkey for instance. In many instances the hesitation to tax the agricultural sector is traceable to political factors, although administrative difficulties are generally cited as the explanation. *Either* the rural votes have to be safeguarded – a question of great significance in most democratic, underdeveloped countries in view of their massive rural sectors. *Or* the landed interests constitute an oligarchy powerful enough to block further taxation of the agricultural sector.

Differences in domestic rates of saving

Finally, we should ask whether any significant generalisation can be made about the *overall* rates of domestic savings. It turns out that only negative conclusions can be drawn. There is much variation between countries. International differences in saving performance are quite considerable. Further, they appear to bear no systematic relation to the per capita incomes of countries *or* to their growth rates. This is to be expected. Current incomes depend, among other things, on *past*, rather than present savings. Nor are current growth rates in income exclusively a function of domestic savings; foreign savings for instance, can adequately substitute for a shortfall in domestic savings. Yet, it is important not to forget that higher growth rates, consistent with the elimination of permanent dependence on foreign capital, generally require higher rates of domestic saving.

7 Human resources

Economists have tended in the past to concentrate too much on the inability of underdeveloped countries to accumulate *capital*. Only recently have they come to consider *human* resources with the respect that the subject undoubtedly deserves. Indeed, as always, the pendulum has swung to the other extreme: it is already fashionable and part of the 'new' orthodoxy to underplay the role of capital and to explain underdevelopment essentially in terms of the limitations imposed by inadequate human resources.

What are these resources? Several attributes of human populations can be distinguished. The qualities most relevant to the problems of underdevelopment are considered most conveniently under four main heads: 1 entrepreneurial ability; 2 skilled manpower; 3 the state of administration; and 4 national character.

Entrepreneurial ability

The capacity and willingness to undertake risks and to innovate in economic activity constitute the ingredients of entrepreneurship. These qualities are clearly important for economic progress. Growth in income is vitally dependent on the rate at which opportunities for technical and economic innovation are perceived and seized. The British industrial revolution was founded on the ingenuity of entrepreneurs in practically all forms of economic activity. Technical progress swiftly overtook many sectors: the spinning-jenny, Crompton's mule and Watt's steam engine are among the principal landmarks of eighteenth century economic history. These inventions were readily adopted by entrepreneurs in their search for bigger profits. Agriculture also underwent a rapid transition. The combination of inventions, their exploitation by innovating entrepreneurs and their dissemination through the investment of others in them, was the key to Britain's accelerated growth through the early decades of the last century.

How are the underdeveloped countries of today placed with respect to this crucial resource? It is impossible to be definitive. But by and large there seems little room for pessimism. We have already noted the capacity even of tradition-bound peasants to respond to profitability by way of investments and changes in crop pattern. To this must be added the widely observed excursions by sections of the population into trade, real estate speculation, financial activity and transport. Anthropologists have recorded instances, such as in Gujarat (India) and in Guatemala, where the entrepreneurial tendency is so widespread as to dominate the entire character of these societies. On the other hand, they have also come across social groups and entities with a basically stagnant outlook on life – as in some Polynesian islands and among Bantu peasants. How far, however, these varying characteristics are themselves conditioned by history and institutional circumstances is a question of considerable significance. The rapidity with which entrepreneurial abilities have mushroomed in certain planned economies such as India and Colombia, in response to opportunities for earning profits, suggests that perhaps this type of human resource is unlikely to be a significant brake on development in the long run.

The efficiency and pattern of entrepreneurship in a society are correctly considered by historians and sociologists as a function of prevailing social values and institutions. The impact of the *Protestant ethic* on the supply of entrepreneurs in Western European industrial revolutions is generally recognised today. The role of *alienation* from society of specific groups, which assert themselves through entrepreneurship, has also been important. Quakers and Jews have provided in European (Catholic and Protestant) industrialisations much of the required entrepreneurial talent. In many instances, foreign *immigrants*, outside the accepted social strata, have provided the entrepreneurial thrust. The impressive performance of Lebanese and Syrians initially as traders and later as industrialists in Brazil, of Asia Minor refugees in Greece, of Christians in Syria and Lebanon, of Chinese immigrants and settlers in South Asia, of Indian settlers in Mauritius and the West Indies, and of Spanish and French entrepreneurs in Mexico is well known. In contrast, historians have also recorded examples where

A cement factory in the industrial suburbs
of Tunis. Such enterprises in underdeveloped
countries create a demand for both
managerial and operative skills,
as well as for a steady industrial
labour force.

high status and *respectability* for the entrepreneurial classes have
facilitated the entry of fresh talent into this group; this has been
the case in the United States, for instance, from the earliest times.

The underdeveloped countries generally exhibit an entrepreneurial preference for non-industrial enterprise. This is due to
the economic fact that the prospects for successful industrial
activity are less certain in these areas. Trade, land speculation and
moneylending are spheres in which both custom and economic
organisation reduce the degree of risk and in which a quick and
large profit is generally possible. However, it must be noted that
these entrepreneurial classes often *do* turn to industrial activity in
the underdeveloped areas when rapid expansion occurs and the risk
of industrial activity is thereby reduced. Often, under protective
State measures (such as tariffs, safeguarded markets and subsidies), the relative hazards of industrial entrepreneurship are
diminished and the very same classes that preferred the traditional
forms of entrepreneurship enter the industrial sector. This has been

observed time and again. Indeed, in many underdeveloped countries which have experienced sustained expansion, the trading classes have produced the leading industrial entrepreneurs: as with Marwaris, Parsis and Gujaratis in India and with the Lebanese and Syrians in Brazil. Where, however, the State has *either* failed in its attempts to encourage entrepreneurship *or* preferred not to undertake them, industrial enterprise has been *initiated* by the government itself through the enlargement of the public sector. During the last decade in India the State has directly entered the field of production in many heavy industries of social value, government employees (civil servants and industrial managers) acting as entrepreneurs but without the attendant risks. Indeed this tradition is very old: the early decades of Japanese industrialisation in the Meiji era were marked by active governmental participation in economic activity, followed by the hand-over of several successful enterprises to the private sector.

The relative merits of these different ways in which entrepreneurship may be generated or enlarged in the underdeveloped countries is a question of some importance. It is also one which has attracted controversy: the role of the State is an issue which pointedly divides political economists. We shall have to revert to it when we consider the methods by which the process of transformation in underdeveloped economies can be started and accelerated.

Skilled personnel

Entrepreneurial ability is not enough by itself. Skilled manpower must also be available. Factories need to be managed and machines need to be operated. Banks have to be staffed and buses and trains have to be run. Agricultural techniques must be learnt and in turn taught to innumerable peasants. The need for trained and skilled personnel cuts across all sectors of economic activity.

Managerial skills are among the scarcest in underdeveloped countries. This is due largely to the trading and speculative background of the entrepreneurs. While these men often show great financial and commercial acumen, they rarely exhibit the capacity to organise and manage *producing* units. The modern science of *operations research* has thrown into relief many instances of managerial inefficiency in the underdeveloped countries. Several firms in India, for example, made great economies by appreciating that labour could be substituted for capital in a number of ways. In a textile plant, it was found that operatives continually left their looms for refreshments and so on, the machinery thus remaining idle. A scheme under which extra hands were employed so that they could step in and operate the looms during these periods was found to bring substantial savings. In view of the relative cheapness of Indian labour it was apparently more economical to leave men rather than machinery idle. A keen manager looks out for such economies, instead of slavishly imitating traditional or foreign practice. Quality control and production programming are among the modern techniques of management which are quite unheard of in many of the poor areas. It is perhaps here that foreign investment, which is usually accompanied by foreign management at least in the early stages, plays a significant role in demonstrating the possibility and profitability of more scientific methods.

Operative skills are of equal importance. The advanced countries have built up, over time, a number of institutions which provide a continuous flow of the skills which their industrialised economies need. These range from technical colleges, producing a large variety of expertise, to apprenticeships at the factories. There are few such institutions in the underdeveloped countries. Their educational systems are geared, for the most part, to creating Arts graduates, equipped with culture rather than with technical knowledge. This is not irrational, as these economies are organised today. In their present state of development, most of the underdeveloped countries are not capable of absorbing significantly more technical personnel than their systems turn out. But this is *not* to deny that these institutions will have to be rapidly created and expanded if expansion programmes are to be sustained.

There is no reason to suppose that these changes will be held

Figure 17. *Technical assistance expenditures in 1961.* The role of the United States and France has so far been predominant in bilateral programmes. Multilateral assistance, as a proportion of total expenditure, has been barely over 6%.

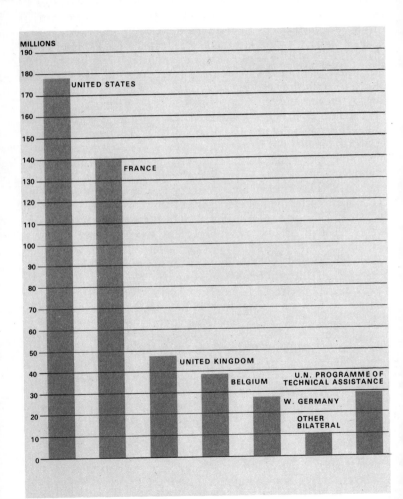

MILLIONS

UNITED STATES

FRANCE

UNITED KINGDOM

BELGIUM

W. GERMANY

OTHER BILATERAL

U.N. PROGRAMME OF TECHNICAL ASSISTANCE

up owing to the 'technical ineptitude' of the inhabitants of the poor nations. Capacity to learn the skills required in an industrialised society is *not* confined to any particular race or region. Nor must we forget the existence today of international agencies which promote the international flow of skilled manpower. The role that the migration of skilled artisans from Europe played in the industrialisation of the United States is now being partially fulfilled by the technical assistance programmes sponsored by multilateral and bilateral agencies.

Bilateral technical assistance alone has doubled since the second half of the 1950's, and in 1961 stood at over $400 million (see figure 17). These programmes have also played an important part in financing the foreign *training* of operatives from the underdeveloped countries. Indeed, a great deal of the financial aid tied to specific projects is being currently combined with technical assistance for setting up and operating the plants – which includes training for indigenous technicians in the donor countries.

The state of administration

While entrepreneurial, managerial and technical skills are important, it is equally necessary to enquire how the underdeveloped countries are placed with regard to administrative ability. This is a very large question which is underlined by the tragic experience of countries such as Indonesia and the (former) Belgian Congo. There is a remarkable contrast between the competent administrative machinery of India and Pakistan – a fortuitous legacy of the Civil Service carefully built up during British rule – and the inadequate, inefficient and halting administrations which are general in many South Asian and African countries.

Bad administration has many implications. It frequently leads to corruption. This in turn slows up work; and the delays are economically damaging. People's moral fibre is corroded, which in turn breeds cynicism and frustrates the growth of the spirit of enthusiasm and idealism which are vital to expansion programmes. The rot

An apparently rickety but none the less effective structure, typical of the Chinese tin mines in Malaya. The overseas Chinese are generally enterprising, thrifty and industrious – qualities which are characteristic of people who work in an alien, challenging environment.

seeps into practically every national effort: taxation is evaded, energies are spent in bribing officials rather than in creative endeavour, controls create privilege instead of equality and so on. A strong, efficient civil service is a crucial element in the framework necessary for economic growth.

National character

Many analysts would consider the question of 'national character' to be of overriding importance as well. The Chinese, for instance, are believed to be industrious; the Thais are thought to be easygoing; and so on. Within nations also such 'types' are constantly defined. In India, for example, the Punjabis are considered energetic and tremendously hard-working, while the natives of Bengal and the United Provinces are thought to be lazy. In so far as these are valid categories of analysis, they are significant. An

industrious community, for instance, has a far greater prospect for material improvement than a slothful one.

But it is necessary to be clear about the sense in which these are valid distinctions. Frequently these characteristics are the product of an institutional environment which is itself subject to change. Many of the apparently industrious classes and regions reflect social factors like immigration or displacement. The *overseas* Chinese and Indians are particularly hard-working and accumulate savings rapidly; but this is surely the result of their operation in an alien environment and partly of the fact that those who emigrate are the enterprising ones. In the more placid environment of their own societies, they do not display the same degree of industry. Similarly, the quality of honesty, essential to good administration, has been known to be severely and quickly undermined when governments have rashly multiplied intervention and controls beyond the capacity of their administrative systems. Thus, while generalisations concerning national character are possible, it is important not to build analysis on them without remembering that they are intimately connected with social and economic institutions. Further, the incidence of different national attributes such as honesty and industriousness, which bear directly on economic prospects, is naturally uneven and random between different underdeveloped countries. There is little that economic analysis can contribute to its study.

There are, naturally, also other qualities of populations which bear on the question of development. The level of literacy, for example, will affect the receptivity of people to new ideas; here the underdeveloped countries are rather badly placed, as we have seen earlier (chapter 2). This is again not an innate but an acquired characteristic; but the fact remains that, as of now, most under-developed countries do not have the advantages that widespread literacy brings. Aside from literacy, the quality and orientation of education are also important; they can condition the objectives which society sets for itself. The question of the quality of human resources is ultimately an extensive one, with many dimensions.

Figure 18. *Decline in crude death rate in eighteen underdeveloped areas, 1920–54.*
1920–4 is taken as base and the *average* death rate for the selected countries is taken.
The countries are: Barbados, Costa Rica, Ceylon, Cyprus, Egypt, El Salvador,
Fiji Islands, Jamaica, Malaya, Mauritius, Mexico, Panama, Philippines, Puerto Rico,
Surinam, Taiwan, Thailand and Trinidad–Tobago. There has been an
unprecedented fall in the death rate in several underdeveloped countries in this
period, a prospect which faces others.

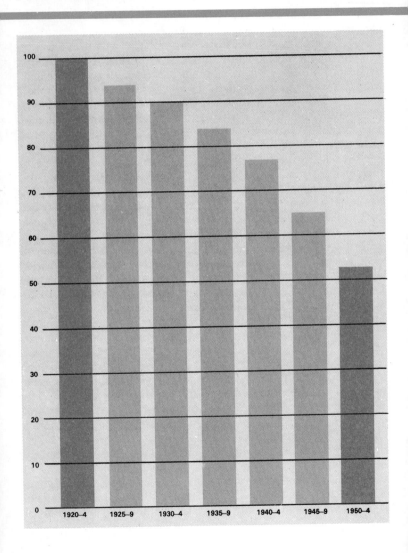

8 The population perspective

Although the *quality* of the population is no less significant, the question of its sheer *size* has been receiving greater attention. According to many demographers, the population of the world is growing at a rate that promises unprecedented disaster. Whether one agrees with this gloomy prediction or not, it can be safely asserted that the growth of population in the underdeveloped areas is an alarming prospect. The reason is simple: it threatens to nullify the effects of economic expansion on the availability of income *per head*.

It is not as though the net reproductive rate in the underdeveloped areas is uniformly higher than in other parts of the world. Indeed, there are many poor countries with low rates of population growth and several rich countries with high reproductive rates.

The problem is rather that the poor countries with high reproductive rates are in that unfortunate position generally for reasons which threaten to obtain in the remaining underdeveloped areas in the immediate future. High reproductive rates in underdeveloped areas are the result of a drastic fall in the mortality rate, both absolutely and relative to the birth rate. This is in contrast to the recent experience of certain advanced countries where reproductive rates have fallen because of declines in the birth rate, absolutely and relative to the death rate.

In many underdeveloped areas the last five decades have witnessed a striking reduction in the crude death rate (see figure 18). In Chile, for instance, the crude death-rate fell almost 50% in thirty-five years. The reasons for this decline are in contrast to the factors that brought about a significant fall in the mortality rate in the developing countries in the nineteenth century.

Although it is impossible to be definitive, the decline in mortality in the nineteenth century was attributable *primarily* to improving living standards and personal hygiene and relatively less to advances in medicine. Better diets, following upon larger incomes, were important. So was the transition from wool to cotton: cleaner undergarments (from more readily washable cotton) led to better health. Soap, regarded previously as a luxury, came into general

89

Below: an anti-malaria team in India travelling by elephant to reach remote areas. Health improvement lowers the death rate – and accentuates the population problem. *Right*: a string of tribesmen in Chad, in central Africa, suffering from river-blindness. By curing this disease, the World Health Organisation has restored to work people who were a drain on society and thereby improved productivity.

use in the nineteenth century. Social and sanitary reforms followed rapidly on one another: improvement of insanitary housing, filtered water and the elimination of open ditches and cesspools are among the principal landmarks. Medical progress aided but did not outpace this process. Jenner's vaccination against smallpox and the effective use of chlorinated lime water in reducing death in childbirth were among the most powerful advances that affected the mortality rate in the nineteenth century. Such advances, however, are minute compared with the growth in scientific knowledge of disease and its prevention which has dominated the twentieth century.

In contrast, the phenomenal decline in mortality experienced by some of the underdeveloped countries has been largely due to the application of modern science, through public health programmes. In Ceylon, for instance, the use of DDT is estimated to have reduced the death rate, previously stable for fifteen years, by 35% in two years! In Puerto Rico, Madagascar and India, the results have been equally impressive.

While medical measures *can* improve well-being without reducing the death rate, the majority of them necessarily have this effect. The control of infectious and epidemic diseases in particular promises to be a major factor in reducing the mortality rate in many underdeveloped areas. Unfortunately, however, the prospect of a matching fall in the birth rate in these populations is dim. The past experience of underdeveloped areas with striking reductions in mortality is depressing (see figure 19). Declining birth rates have been associated with vast improvements in income levels; the reduction in mortality that the underdeveloped countries are certain to experience, on the other hand, will come earlier than improvement in incomes. Health measures thus threaten to accelerate the growth of population in the poor areas, endangering improvements in their per capita incomes. Here is one of those vicious circles: unless birth rates are controlled, incomes cannot improve materially; unless incomes improve materially, birth rates will not fall. It is the latter half of this proposition that modern science and sociology are attempting to controvert.

Until they succeed, there is an inescapable paradox here. Should society prolong life only to reduce the level of comfort at which it can be led? There is no easy solution to this ethical dilemma.

Figure 19. *Crude birth and death rates for five sample underdeveloped countries 1905–30.* While birth rates have fallen negligibly and have sometimes even increased, decreases in death rates in these countries have been relatively striking during this period. This pattern of differences in the behaviour of death and birth rates has added to the population pressure in several underdeveloped countries. Yet other countries are threatened with this phenomenon.

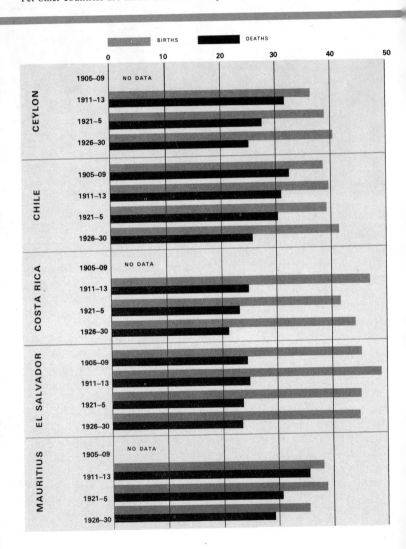

9 Sociological institutions and attitudes

Economic phenomena occur in a social framework. Moreover, they interact with the institutions which make up the social structure. We have already touched upon some of these links: the effects of social valuation on the supply of entrepreneurship, the impact of religious attitudes on population control and the effect of land-holding as a status symbol on savings and investment. But the interactions between economic and social phenomena are so extensive and so pertinent to the study of underdeveloped economies that they require further, separate treatment.

The joint family

In several underdeveloped countries, the concept of the family is more extensive than the nuclear family of Western societies. The institution has a wider connotation, frequently including cousins, uncles and distant relatives in a fairly extended kinship system. Just as kinship organisation varies between societies, so does the scope and nature of the joint family. Among the institution's most recurrent characteristics, the following are significant: *property and income are pooled and inherited as such; similarly, expenditure is not accounted for individually*. Different societies have different rules governing the precise operation of the joint family; but from a wide range of studies in the countries of Africa and South Asia, the essential phenomenon has been observed to be similar.

The historic origin of this institution is obscure. It is frequently, though not invariably, associated with agricultural and subsistence societies and may well have resulted from a desire to avoid excessive fragmentation of the land. Social anthropologists have, however, despaired of making valid inferences about the origins of institutions. They prefer now to study instead the role that these institutions play in the *existing* social framework. This suits our purpose well, since we intend to analyse the impact of the joint family on the economic system.

One of the most popular theses concerns the supposedly deleterious effect of the joint family on the incentive to work and innovate. The argument rests on the fact that any *one* member of the joint family has to *share* the rewards of his extra work with a large number of relatives, so that the net return to himself or his nuclear family is only a fraction of what his effort brings. The *incentive* to work, therefore, is reduced.

This is not, however, as persuasive an argument as it appears. It presupposes the existence of individualist or nuclear-family economic motivation in a joint-family framework. Just as the father derives utility from the welfare of his children in a nuclear family, so the member of an extended family may well identify his welfare with that of all members of his extended family. Indeed, whenever the individualist and nuclear-family ethic has made its appearance, through accumulation or economic change, the joint family has undergone rapid change. The urban areas in many underdeveloped countries have witnessed *either* the disappearance of the joint family *or* the *de facto* separation of property, income and expenditure while common *residence* alone is continued.

The popular argument also overlooks the significant fact that many social *valuations* which centre on the joint family frequently provide a powerful incentive to work and accumulate wealth. In many African and Asian societies, for instance, a person's social prestige depends on the number of extended family members and dependants he supports and the level of comfort at which he supports them. In fact, it may well be that the tendency to nepotism in many underdeveloped countries has a sociological foundation in the institution of the joint family!

The joint family has, on the other hand, several advantages which pertain to the state of underdevelopment. In countries and societies where no other form of insurance and social security is available, the joint family has traditionally offered security to its disabled and weaker members. This has its economic advantages. Instances are known where talented children have been educated by the joint family although the father may individually be a drag on the family, where risky innovations have been attempted thanks to the security of the joint family in the event of failure. Indeed, in the overcrowded urban centres of the poor countries, wherever the joint family has disintegrated, the economic cost of the security that government or industry now has to provide is fairly high.

The caste system and economic mobility

The institution of the caste system, prevalent especially in India though also in varying degrees in other parts of Asia, has also received much attention. Castes are frequently endogamous and they are generally believed to be village-centred. It is also widely thought that they are functional in terms of occupation; tailors belong to one caste, carpenters to another and so on. Occupational and geographic mobility of labour is therefore considered to be one of the casualties of the system.

This argument is substantially correct. However, it is necessary to remember, as many recent sociological studies have shown, that castes *have* changed their occupational classification in the past. Also, labour mobility between regions has been observed since the earliest times: few castes are exclusively village-based and most of them in fact stretch across large parts of the country. Occupational mobility, further, cannot have been impaired very significantly because many castes necessarily permit a *range* of occupations: this is itself a function of the economic fact noted earlier – namely, the lack of complete specialisation in work in many of the under-developed countries.

The caste system, again, is unlikely to impede seriously the growth of a modern industrial labour force necessary for an industrialising economy. In the urban areas, whether one refers to the large rural towns or to greater metropolitan centres, the caste system tends to dissolve in the anonymity and flux that departure from a rural life invariably brings. In the plants and factories, in trains and buses, it is impossible to differentiate castes and follow their dictates. The city and the machine are the great levellers. This is *not* to claim, however, that castes cease to play any part at all. It usually takes three generations before links with the village and the

The marriage of two employees of Nagasaki's
public works department. The man in the place
of honour behind the couple is not the
father of the bride but the manager
of the department. This picture typifies the
paternalism of Japanese industry.

caste begin to loosen. Immigrants usually settle in areas where their
relations and caste-fellows live; thus there are caste-settlements,
congregations, and segregated sections in different parts of the city
much as there are Chinatowns or Jewish ghettos, or the Negro
Harlem and the Puerto Rican quarter in New York. It is frequently
a matter of security, of clinging to old roots and seeking familiar
faces in an alien and hostile environment. Such clannishness rarely
outlasts more than one or two generations. It merely delays the
disintegration of the caste system.

But the caste system *has* been found to continue by *adapting*
itself to new social and political conditions. And this has happened
in many interesting ways. Trade-union activity organised along
caste lines has sometimes been observed, though it is a matter for
conjecture how long this can continue in an industrial environment.
More significantly, caste has become a major *political* factor in
democratic elections. In India, parties soon found that putting up a
candidate belonging to the majority caste was an important factor
in winning elections. While this would normally have been inimical
to the growth of secular democracy, it is interesting to note that the
perniciousness of caste has now been *de facto* eliminated from the
political scene. Candidates from *all* parties now tend to be chosen
from the dominant castes, thereby *neutralising* the caste factor and
leaving the political choice ultimately to be made by the electorate
on non-caste grounds!

The resilience of the caste system, demonstrated by some of the
modern forms in which it appears, reminds one of the way in which
the Japanese factory has assimilated the extended family system.
Labour recruitment in Japanese firms is apparently for life and it is
not customary for a worker to move to a different firm or for a
firm to poach another's labour force. On a visit to a large chemical
plant in Osaka, I was impressed by the obvious youth of practically
all skilled operatives and enquired the reason. The answer was that
the firm itself was very young! The factories are thus operated in
Japan much like families. The labour force identifies itself with the
firm and the management literally has to conduct itself towards the

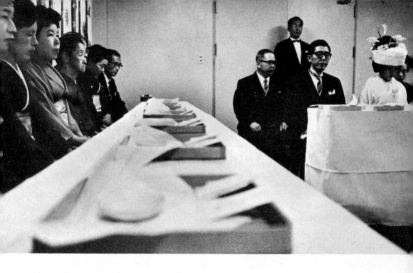

workers in that spirit. Inefficient workers, for example, do not get fired; they are just not promoted. The social security of the extended family is thus available inside the modern factory!

Religious and other social attitudes

Values and attitudes are as significant as traditional, social institutions. The sociologists talk of the 'world-view' that a society has and its implications for human and social action. In their effect on enterprise, supply of effort, accumulation of wealth and numerous other economic phenomena the social valuations which motivate people are quite important.

Religion is admittedly influential in this respect. We have previously referred to the role of the Protestant ethic in the European industrial revolutions of the late eighteenth and early nineteenth centuries. The effect of Roman Catholicism on fertility has also been noted. Equally significant are many of the traditional religious tenets in the underdeveloped areas of today. *Parts* of Hinduism in India and Buddhism in Ceylon, Cambodia and Thailand inculcate a *fatalistic* attitude towards life. This has ecological meaning too: in a subsistence peasant economy, with primitive techniques, subject to the ravages of weather, an acceptance of the fatalistic theory of life is natural. A negative, other-life-oriented, non-materialistic bias can also be found in the religions of these South Asian countries.

But these teachings frequently have to compete with other aspects and segments of Hinduism which are strongly oriented to action and the present world. Some of the most popular and eloquently phrased scriptures of the Hindus talk of renunciation *not* of action itself but of *involvement* in the action, in its results, in its fruits. Action in fact is exhorted, recommended and required.

Religion frequently intervenes *directly* in economic organisation. The Moslem injunction against usury has raised considerable difficulties in Islamic countries. Interest rates perform the economic function of rationing capital and making it available for the most advantageous uses; they can even encourage the accumulation of savings. However, in orthodox Moslem countries it is sometimes quite difficult to charge or raise interest rates without causing political disturbance.

There is an interesting parallel here with the practice of communism which, in many ways, performs the essential sociological functions of religious faith for its atheistic followers. Marxism denounces interest rates as vehemently as the Moslem Prophet did! According to Marx, labour alone is the source of value; rent and interest are merely forms of exploitation. In conformity with this rigid but fallacious doctrine, the Soviet planners dare not use an interest rate in their economic calculation and allocation of capital to different uses. Under the pressure of economic realities, however, they have begun lately to use the so-called 'pay-off period' technique which is really a backdoor method of introducing the rate of interest into their planning. Suppose that one type of steel mill, carrying investment worth 10,000,000 roubles, can recoup the sum in ten years whereas another, costing 15,000,000 roubles, can recoup it in fifteen years. The *difference* between the two alternatives, then, is an additional investment of 5,000,000 roubles for the second mill and a further recoupment period of five years. The Soviet planners may then rule out the more expensive steel mill because the *additional* recoupment period is considered *too long*. But this itself means that a rate of interest has been used implicitly. If the recoupment or the pay-off period must not be greater than four years, for instance, it implies that the capital must produce approximately 25% annually before it can be sanctioned. This is virtually the same thing as using a 25% rate of interest!

Communist practice has in this instance got round the doctrine of Marxism while paying lip service to it. More difficult, however, has been the task of getting round the equally rigid Marxist view on population control. Writing essentially in an industrial environment, Marx thought it politically necessary to link the poverty and distress of the proletariat around him so firmly to the forces of history and the intrinsic nature of capitalism as to rule out the utilitarian exhortations for birth control as irrelevant and mischievous. As with many Marxist tenets which have become out of date in the world of today, however, the ruthless dismissal of birth control is a serious handicap to the overpopulated, underdeveloped countries of communist persuasion. The schizophrenic, fleeting acceptance and sudden rejection of a population policy by China in the last decade are a pointed reminder of the limitation imposed by ideological and religious values upon economic action.

Finally, one further effect of social valuation on political economy may be noted. The attitudes towards profit, accumulation and lavish consumption vary between countries. In the few under-developed countries with genuine, political leanings to the left, the attitude towards profits is borrowed from the historic and by-gone experience of foreign monopolies and domestic rentiers. The resulting contempt for profits stands in the way of a rational planning of the public sector projects in these countries. In India, Pakistan, Ceylon and elsewhere, public corporations have until very recently been reluctant to make large profits, regardless of whether they operate road transport or manufacture heavy machinery. The consequent under-pricing of products leads to fiscal difficulties, as well as to excessive use and wastage of scarce and valuable commodities. Indeed in India, since the public sector enterprises manufacture materials which are used mostly by private corporations, the profits foregone by the government accrue instead to private entrepreneurs!

Attitudes towards accumulation can also be deleterious. If thrift is not valued but equated with greed, savings may prove difficult to secure. The phenomenal rate of growth of G.N.P. in Japan before the Second World War is to be attributed, among other things, to the fact that the Japanese preferred the traditional, modest patterns of consumption and did not go massively for the consumer durables that were flooding the Western markets at the time. In consequence, Japanese households could accumulate a great deal, and without social opprobrium.

Attitudes towards luxury consumption can also be relevant. The mild inflation and investment boom that usually attends acceleration in the growth of incomes tends to lead to high profits. They are also generally accompanied by taxation and other stiff and unwelcome measures of austerity. If the profits were to be spent on luxury consumption, this would create very great tensions. A social valuation, therefore, in favour of accumulation and against lavish consumption, will prevent the difficulties that are otherwise inherent in a situation of rapid expansion. Here again, the contrasting experience of Japan, where ostentatious consumption was at a minimum, and of India where it has been extensive and disruptive, is revealing.

Perhaps we can conclude on an optimistic note. While social attitudes and institutions undoubtedly impinge on economic possibilities, we have also observed how economic changes frequently manage to alter and adjust the attitudes and institutions themselves. Time and again, sociologists have studied the effect of development on social structure only to record that ultimately few changes can be long delayed by social factors. In a stimulating recent analysis of the impact of irrigation on two villages in South India, a social anthropologist has found that in the village where economic improvement and change were possible without change in the social structure, they occurred without such disruption; but in the village where economic development demanded social change, institutions did adapt themselves. Perhaps this is not typical; but it seems eminently plausible. And in it lies the cause for optimism.

10 Environmental constraints

The social and economic characteristics of the underdeveloped countries *constrain* the prospects for their economic expansion. The capacity to save in these countries affects their ability to invest. Their future export earnings are important since they have to be stepped up to increase their capacity to import the capital goods, raw materials and consumer goods which are the prerequisites to growth. A large number of skills and an industrial working force have to be made available to operate the factories and plants which will cause incomes to grow. Administrators have to be found and trained to carry out the plans formulated by governments.

In these and many other respects, the current social and economic structure of the underdeveloped countries, discussed so far, is a sobering reminder of the difficulties that attend the task of transforming these economies. Clearly, no simple solutions exist; the problem will have to be tackled simultaneously on many fronts. Mere aid from the advanced countries, for instance, will not do the trick; unless an efficient political and administrative machinery exists, and unless well-formulated plans are devised to absorb the inflow of these funds, they will go substantially to waste, as indeed they have done in many underdeveloped countries. Population control will not be feasible unless religious attitudes which make its active adoption politically explosive, as in Roman Catholic countries, are appreciated and tackled. Export earnings will not increase unless the advanced countries initiate necessary changes in the international economy. Expenditure, organisation and education are needed on many fronts, both at the national and at international levels, if efforts towards development are to be reasonably successful.

These important lessons of history and experience need to be fully learnt. It is only against the background of the social and economic conditions obtaining in the underdeveloped areas that the problems of transition to higher and sustained growth can be usefully analysed. Those analysts who ignore this prescription remind us of the typically well-meaning but ignorant British

101

official in early nineteenth century India, as described by a brilliant-
ly perceptive commentary of the time:

> Every man writes as much as he can, and quotes Montesquieu, and Hume,
> and Adam Smith, and speaks as if he were living in a country where people
> were free and governed themselves. Most of their papers might have been
> written by men who were never out of England, and their projects are
> nearly as applicable to that country, as to India . . . [There is none to be
> dreaded] half so much as an able Calcutta civilian, whose travels are limited
> to two or three hundred miles, with a hookah in his mouth, some good but
> abstract maxims in his head, the Regulations in his right hand, the Com-
> pany's Charter in his left, and a quire of wire-woven foolscap before him.

Now that we have surveyed the principal economic and social
features of the underdeveloped countries, we are in a better position
to consider the national and international actions that will facilitate
the process of economic expansion. We turn first to the internal
aspects in Part Three. International measures are treated later in
Part Four.

The process of transformation

A field under cultivation in the Golden Star People's Commune in Shansi province, north China. Collectivisation of agriculture, whether or not it has proved successful, is ruled out in most underdeveloped countries as a method of improving output, since it is in conflict with non-economic objectives such as the freedom of labour.

11 Developmental targets and methods

Economic expansion on a firm, continuing, sustained and permanent basis is naturally the overriding objective of most underdeveloped countries today. However, the task of formulating programmes to achieve it immediately raises fundamental questions. Are there not *other objectives*, different from the desire to increase the rate of growth of G.N.P. per capita, which these governments share? If so, might there not be a conflict between these diverse aims? How could such conflicts be resolved? Again, in attaining these objectives might there not be certain social and political *constraints* on the actions of these governments? Might not certain *methods* (such as collectivisation of agriculture either of the Soviet variety or as in the Chinese Communes) be ruled out in some underdeveloped countries though not in others? These questions cannot be brushed aside; they affect and condition the advice and prescriptions that social analysts can offer to the developing countries.

Governments in fact have a wide range of objectives. A high rate of growth of income, an egalitarian distribution of income, fuller employment, the development of backward regions, the creation of strategic industries and the reduction of reliance on foreign trade are among the principal economic and 'non-economic' aims that animate most governments.

This is indeed a large assortment of objectives and few of them can be simultaneously achieved. A tax policy, for example, which is geared to the redistribution of income in favour of the poor may reduce the growth of G.N.P.; the poor may save less while the rich save more, so that the net effect of the redistributive policy may be a reduction in the national savings and hence in investment. Again, a policy of developing backward regions may involve the use of scarce resources in areas where the returns are low. Hence the result may be a low level of current G.N.P. The development of backward regions would thus be in conflict with an increase in the national income.

The conflict may even be between the *same* objective at *different* points in time. Thus a policy of promoting full employment in the

Figure 20. *Choice of a programme of current employment and income from a set of alternative combinations of each.* Assuming that the authorities are interested in current employment and income, the planners can work out the alternative combinations of these two objectives that are *feasible*, given the resources and technology in the country. From these, the authorities can then make a definite choice (as explained in the text).

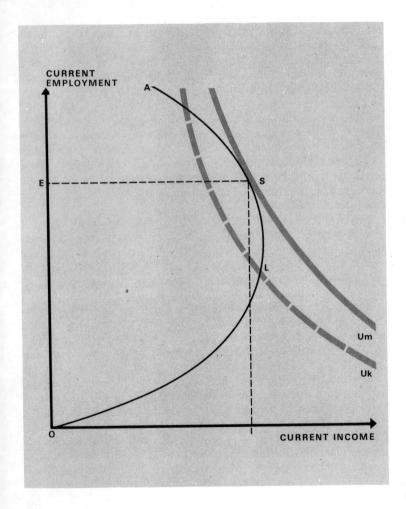

immediate future may be an obstacle to full employment later. Suppose everyone was employed right away in a typical, over-populated country such as Turkey or Indonesia. This would mean that jobs would have to be created although complementary factors such as spades, shovels, buses, looms and factories were not available. The bulk of the people would thus have to be 'employed' in unproductive ways. Two conductors might be put on a bus where only one is necessary; and so on. The result would be an inflation of the wage-bill at the expense of profits. This would cut into the nation's capacity to save and severely impair its capacity to accumulate capital. In consequence there would be a correspondingly slower rate of expansion of those very co-operating factors (such as machinery and equipment) that would otherwise have led to genuine employment of greater numbers in the future. More jobs today would then conflict with more jobs tomorrow. This is indeed a dilemma which recurs everywhere. More consumption today means less consumption tomorrow; and so on.

If then these conflicts between objectives can occur both at one point of time *and* between different time periods, what is to be done? The objectives will naturally have to be weighed one against the other. Assume that current employment and income are the two targets which interest the authorities. Suppose that, for this economy, the technical possibilities are such that (see figure 20) OSA represents the combination of employment and income levels from which a choice can be made. Presented with this set of possible choices, the government (exercising social discretion) may select position S, implying an income of OI units and employment of OE units.

Economists, however, like to think of this decision-making process as one where the authorities *maximise* social satisfaction. In interpreting the decision this way, the economist puts against the possibility curve OSA, another schedule, such as Um, which represents a locus of different combinations of income and employment levels among which the society is *indifferent*. Since point S lies on the schedule Um, the society, in choosing S, also derives the welfare level measured at Um. This welfare level is *also* the maximum feasible because, *given the possibilities measured by OSA*, the society *cannot* do better than at Um (although it can do *worse*, as at Uk by choosing L). Not everyone would agree that this description of social choice was valid. Certainly, few governments would be prepared or able to specify their preferences in the way suggested. However they could certainly make a choice when presented with concrete alternatives to choose from.

Conflicts over time can also be resolved in this way. In principle, it is possible to calculate the impact of different policies with respect to any assigned objective or set of objectives. If income were the objective, two different policies, pursued efficiently, might yield two streams of income over time, I and II (in figure 21), from which a choice would have to be made. The political authorities might make a straightforward choice, faced with these concrete alternatives. But many economists again like to see the decision as resulting from some form of welfare-maximising process. This however raises some complex, though interesting questions. How is one to evaluate and compare paths which have necessarily two dimensions: income and time? Should the accrual of income later be weighed less than the accrual of income earlier? A system of time-discount is popular with economists, but seems to have little justification: after all, the very purpose of prior calculation is to avoid the kind of myopia that the use of a time-discount rate implies. Again, how should the time-period be set, over which the income streams are to be compared? Changing the time-horizon may reverse the choice: with a time-horizon short enough to be to the left of the intersection point, stream II is indisputably better; on the other hand, with a longish time horizon sufficiently to the right, stream I may be superior. These and other problems are interesting; there is no single answer to them.

The diversity of objectives is matched by the large number of methods by which most of the objectives can be achieved. Agricultural output can be increased, for instance, through land reform, price stabilisation, irrigation or some combination of these and

Women making clothes for the poor under a special employment scheme in Tunis. The question of whether to have unemployment for a time with its consequent hardships or full employment immediately at a low level of productivity, thus jeopardising the chances of genuine full employment later, is a dilemma facing the governments of most underdeveloped countries.

other measures. Many of these alternatives will have different political and social connotations. And these differences are all significant.

An underdeveloped country, wedded to democratic ways and the rule of law, is not in a position to adopt the draconian measures that communist countries readily resort to, such as the subordination of trade unions and the direction of labour. Again, an oligarchy of vested interests will not entertain economic measures which threaten its privileged position. This happens typically in some Latin American countries where, largely for political reasons, inflation is preferred to taxation, though it is an inferior method of financing investments. In Chile, inflation of over 50% per annum has been tolerated by the authorities, under pressure from business groups which were permitted to borrow money from the banking system to finance their excessive expenditure; these groups have also been the beneficiaries of the inflation since rising prices increase profits. Land reform has been held up in many countries, and has sometimes been nominally put on the legislative statutes only to be generally evaded in practice, because of the preponderance of landed interests in both the legislative and executive branches of the government.

Having noted this, however, there is little that the social analyst can add. Where he *can* help, however, is in resolving the sterile and theological controversy that has sprung up around the question of the *role of the State* in promoting development.

There are two important things to note in this respect; both are rooted in experience and the lessons that history suggests. To begin with, the role of the State in most of the *laissez-faire*, 'capitalist' economies of the West is far larger than is commonly realised. And this itself is in conformity with the utilitarian prescriptions of Bentham (which provide the foundations of *laissez-faire* philosophy) and the teachings of political economy from the time of its origin with Adam Smith's *The Wealth of Nations* nearly two centuries ago. *Laissez-faire* has always presupposed *active* governmental intervention at several levels. For instance, 'trust-busting' in the United States and anti-monopoly legislation in Great Britain are governmental actions *required* to make *laissez-faire* (in the economic system) socially beneficial. This is frequently lost sight of, because of the tendency to approach the problem of State action in black-and-white terms.

In the second place, history seems to underline the importance of State action in engineering and assisting the process of take-off in developing economies. It has even been argued recently that the more backward an economy when it proceeds to modernise itself,

Figure 21. *Alternative time-paths of income which are technologically open to the economy and from which a choice must be made by the authorities.* Assuming the authorities are aiming at income, the planners can work out alternative time-paths which are possible, given the resources available. The authorities can then choose one; and the plan will embody the programme which generates that particular time-profile of income.

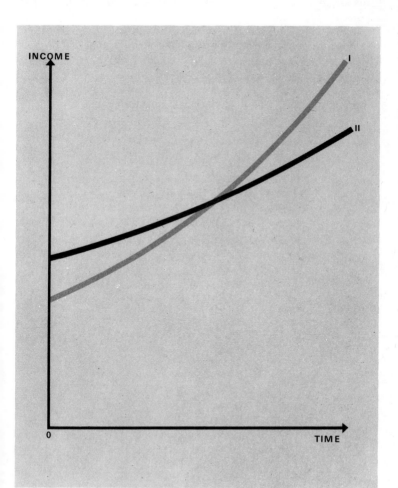

the larger tends to be the range of necessary action by the State: a proposition that seems to be sustained by English, Prussian and Japanese experience.

Clearly, therefore, it makes no sense to take up a doctrinal stand on the question of the role of the State in the developmental process. The important question is to judge whether any specific *type* of State action, while advantageous from the economic point of view, is likely to impinge on social values. This necessarily enforces a pragmatic approach to the question of State action.

12 Raising the resources

All kinds of resources are obviously necessary for accelerating economic development. We propose, however, to focus here on the savings which are crucial for the accumulation of capital. Other resources, with some notable exceptions, also largely depend on the availability of savings: the exceptions are administrative, entrepreneurial and organisational resources which cannot necessarily be created with savings and the lack of which may prove to be the limiting bottlenecks in development in many underdeveloped areas.

Savings ultimately will have to be raised through domestic taxation in these countries, both because the required increase in savings is so large *and* because there is no other way of increasing them fairly and efficiently. In many developing countries, the ratio of savings to G.N.P. will have to be raised more than threefold: from levels of 4–8% to 15–20%. This is a drastic change and is in fact even more demanding than it appears to be since the savings out of the *incremental* incomes will have to be even *larger* than the desired, high, average savings ratios. Let us suppose that the average savings rate is to be raised from 10% to 15% on an income of 100 roubles. Let us further suppose that income doubles. The rate of savings on 100 roubles was 10% or 10 roubles. But 10% of the second 100 roubles (10 roubles) means that no increase in the rate of saving has taken place. To obtain a 15% rate of savings (30 of the 200 roubles), it is necessary to save 20 of the second 100 roubles. Thus the savings from the incremental income (the second 100 roubles) will have to be at a rate of 20% to raise the average savings rate from 10% to 15%. The large increases in savings that are quickly demanded just cannot, and indeed have not, come from *voluntary* savings in the underdeveloped countries.

The only serious alternative to taxation therefore is inflation, also a method of forced savings. It is, however, an inferior instrument for several reasons. Its incidence is arbitrary; the price rise, in practice, can be uneven and unpredictable in its structure. It also frequently hurts the weakest sections of the community: the retired and aged, orphans and widows, wage-earners, in fact all classes enjoying incomes fixed with varying firmness at a monetary sum whose real value depreciates with rising prices. As a long-run method of financing development, it is also inefficient. Inflation usually transfers incomes to the richer sections via increased profits; and profits tend to get dissipated partially through conspicuous consumption. Taxation, on the other hand, would channel the diverted incomes entirely to productive use by the government. Furthermore, inflation can create difficulties in a country's external economic relations. If prices rise, the country may find itself unable to sell its goods in foreign markets while its own market would find ready suppliers from abroad. The result would be a deficit in the country's balance of payments, with a continuing loss of reserves and possible subsequent devaluation of its currency's exchange value. This can be an unsettling sequence of events, with deleterious effects. Indeed, most governments, faced with balance of payments difficulties, have tended to adopt restrictive monetary policies: credit rationing leads to reduced outlays and investments, the resulting unemployment and reduction of income leading to reduced demand for imports and a consequent restoration of balance in the country's international accounts. The inflation thus leads to unemployment and loss of income, as most governments are constituted and operate. Taxation thus remains the only desirable method of raising the required savings.

Taxation, however, does not merely raise revenue and increase savings. It affects incentives; and it may influence administrative and social morality in certain circumstances. Political economists of the *laissez-faire* persuasion are inclined to lay particular stress on the adverse effects of taxation on incentives. If income tax, for instance, is high, it is claimed that it will reduce the amount of work done. This may well be so; but it is neither inevitable nor overwhelmingly probable. Income tax has two effects: it reduces the net income (after tax) and it makes it less profitable to give up leisure and do more work. The effect on income will prompt greater effort: the lost income has to be regained. On the other hand, the substitution (of work for leisure) effect will lead to smaller effort because the reward for work is reduced. The two effects thus work in opposite directions. The supply schedule of labour may then have the paradoxical property that, as the wage rate falls, the number of hours worked rises (see figure 22). This may be a genuine possibility: many observers of primitive societies even believe it to be the principal characteristic of their labour supply. If this is so, the effect of income tax may well be to increase, rather than reduce, the number of hours worked, (as in figure 22, where a tax which reduces the net wage for the worker from OW_1 to OW_2 also increases the hours worked from OH_1 to OH_2).

In industrialised economies as well, the economic motivation to effort is nowadays largely non-financial. The Vice-President of a corporation works hard to become the President, not because of the extra salary but in pursuit of the status which this position brings. A writer seeks recognition more than mere financial gain. It is extremely unlikely that the incentive to effort among the higher-skilled operatives will be impaired by stiffer taxation. In fact, some recent calculations have shown that the adverse effect of income taxation on the supply of labour is likely to be insignificant in most economies. Governments, therefore, need not allow fear of reduced incentives to deter them from raising taxes in order to increase savings.

More interesting, and also less tractable analytically, is the effect of heavy taxation on administrative and general morality. The critics of taxation are fond of pointing out the corruption in the revenue departments of the underdeveloped countries. They also refer to the widespread evasion and avoidance of taxes. In many countries, such as India, it is customary now to have two sets of accounts, one for the revenue authorities and the other for one's own use. Loopholes actually get built into the tax system itself: capital gains are left largely exempt so that income can be disguised as capital gain; since expenses are deductible for assessment, personal consumption is disguised as corporation expense; and so on. Indeed, some cynics have even argued that the parliaments of most countries, dominated by the richer and privileged

Figure 22. *Supply of labour schedule, linking the hours that a labourer will work to the wage-rate per hour offered to him.*
The schedule (which is explained in the text) illustrates the possibility that a reduction in the wage offered (e.g. by taxation) may increase the number of hours worked.

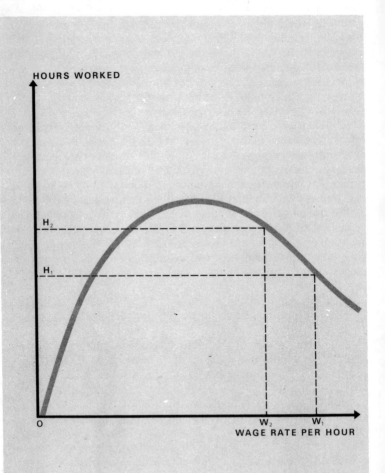

sections of society, would not have legislated the stiff taxation were it not for the fact that enough loopholes would be available to soften its impact! The atmosphere of corruption and dishonesty that surrounds the levels of taxation currently found in several countries is in many respects a genuine problem. But it must be seen as a price that has to be paid to promote economic expansion in the underdeveloped areas.

More serious implications of the evasion and avoidance of taxes relate to 1 the resulting distortion in the relative burden of taxation on different classes *and* 2 the detrimental effect on the accrual of revenue. Take for example the income tax in most countries. The wage and salary earners are easily assessed and, in fact, the deductions are frequently made at the source of income itself: the Pay-As-You-Earn system operates at the factory and office level, so that the pay-cheque is already equal to income *after* taxes. On the other hand, the higher-income groups, deriving the bulk of their income from property and profits, are left with enough loopholes and ways of disguising their real earnings for tax purposes so that their effective tax payments represent probably a smaller proportion of their genuine earnings than is the case with the upper and lower middle classes earning wages and salaries. This *de facto* regressiveness of tax systems, where it exists, is of course unfortunate. But the answer to it is greater vigilance and the elimination (wherever possible) of holes in the tax net. This would also lead to a substantial increase in the revenue of most countries.

Taxable capacity

Is there any limit to the level of taxation that an economy can take? It used to be customary for experts on public finance to talk of the *taxable capacity* of a country. They have now switched to the phrase: *tax potential*. At any moment, the possibility of raising additional taxation will be a function of several social, economic and political factors, among which the following are perhaps the most important.

1 The degree of income inequality would indicate how far taxation could be levied on households without reducing any single household below a given minimum. Thus, the presence of several rich families implies the availability of greater tax potential than their absence. On the other hand, of course, these affluent sections may have the political power to *prevent* the effective imposition of additional taxes – so that greater income inequality may increase the tax potential while impairing the ability to use it!

2 The sector in which incomes are earned also affects the capacity to tax. In the agricultural sector, wherever peasants produce for self-consumption and monetary transactions are infrequent, taxation is relatively difficult and generally avoided. Again, where incomes are earned by petty traders and scattered pedlars of services, the administrative difficulties of taxation may be immense. Indeed, the cost of collection may outweigh the addition to the revenue itself!

3 The rate at which taxation can be *increased* at any moment will also depend on the speed with which the revenue departments can be efficiently expanded. This is a matter of some importance when new *forms* of tax are being introduced and their attendant loopholes have to be traced and plugged.

Choosing the level of taxation

The level of taxation has to be *integrated* into the general programme for development. The purpose of taxation is to increase total savings to the level at which they match the proposed investment. This dictates the way in which the size and pattern of taxation can be calculated. Thus, for example, the Indian Planning Commission begins by estimating the annual investments required to sustain the targeted growth of incomes. From the incomes themselves, an estimate of the voluntary savings by different saver-groups is then made. The gap, if any, between the proposed investment and the forthcoming savings (including *foreign* savings) represents the estimated savings that taxation is required to generate. However, it does *not* necessarily measure the amount of taxation necessary: the latter will be a *larger* sum because taxation will itself reduce the voluntary savings. An income tax, for example, may be paid partly by reducing personal savings, in which case the net addition to national savings which the tax brings will be less than the tax revenue by the amount of the reduced personal savings. This also implies that the level of taxation will itself be dependent on the pattern of taxation that is chosen. If a tax-structure which makes a greater dent on voluntary savings is selected, it will also require a greater tax revenue and a higher tax level to secure the same level of *national* savings.

Pattern of taxation

We are now in a better position to assess certain important issues concerning the pattern of taxation in the underdeveloped countries. These issues relate to four principal questions: agricultural taxation, direct and indirect taxation, and compulsory savings.

The role of agricultural taxation in economic development is twofold. It adds to the total savings. It can also be an important instrument for getting the farmers to bring their output to the market, thereby making it available for industrial workers. Taxation of the farmers increases their marketed surplus of agricultural output because the farmers have to sell this output to pay the taxes. This is not necessarily the case; but it is very probable. This marketable surplus function (which is important for countries with limited trade opportunities and hence limited capacity to import food) has been performed historically in different ways: in Japan by land taxation, in the Soviet Union by forced deliveries and later by ruthless collectivisation of agriculture, and in some countries by raising non-agricultural prices *relative* to agricultural prices (which, by making it more expensive for farmers to buy their industrial consumer goods is likely to increase their marketed output). In many of these instances, governmental action has been required to facilitate the flow of agricultural commodities necessary

to programmes of industrialisation. The role of agricultural taxation in creating this crucial supply of agricultural surpluses, therefore, can be very important.

On the other hand, as we have previously noted, many underdeveloped countries have done little to raise adequate taxation
from the agricultural sector. There were, no doubt, various taxes
in existence several decades ago. For instance, most of these
countries, especially those in Asia (though much less in Africa),
have some form of land taxation, assessed frequently on the annual
value of output per acre and sometimes on the value of the land as
determined in some initial 'settlement'. But in the majority of cases,
the real burden of the taxes has been eroded over time: for instance,
the value of the land at some early date will be an inadequate measure
of its present worth when inflation has occurred, so that taxation
assessed on it will reduce in real terms as time passes and prices
continue to rise. Revisions in these settlements have probably
been held up by inertia reinforced by pressure from landed
interests.

There are so many different types of land taxation that it is
interesting and significant to consider whether any is particularly
suitable to underdeveloped countries planning for rapid expansion.
If a system of land taxation is to be efficient it must fulfil at least
three conditions: 1 it should be sensitive to expansion of agricultural output, so that it yields increasing revenue as the economy
moves forward; 2 it should be equitable as between different sizes
of landholdings, while not undermining the incentive to produce
and invest; and 3 it should not require heavy administrative
expenditure on a recurrent basis. Certain common forms of land
taxation clearly do not fulfil one or the other of these criteria. A
fixed land tax which is not proportionate to the value of output, for
instance, will be easy to administer but also regressive and insensi-
tive to income change.

Perhaps the neatest form in which land taxation can be levied,
requiring limited administrative apparatus on a continuing basis,
is one which has been proposed by many analysts of the Indian

agricultural scene. There would be an initial survey of the land and each holding would be judged in relation to certain characteristics (invariant over the period for which the survey is supposed to be valid: say, twenty years) such as altitude, temperature, fertility and rainfall. Annually, the *overall* tax yield would be determined by the government in relation to the estimated value of output during the year; this aggregate burden would then be *allocated* to individual landholdings in terms of their assigned relative weights (as described earlier).

This tax would thus be sensitive to output changes and also be 'fair' as between landholdings with different advantages. Since the tax on each holding would be related to the *national* output (consistent with the farm's particular advantages and disadvantages) one economic advantage would be the fact that it would build into itself a penalty on the inefficient and a reward for the efficient farms. This, however, might be a political disadvantage, depending on the relative voting strength of the inefficient farms!

The tax could also be made more equitable by introducing the principle of progressivity, so that the tax rate, for holdings of equal weights, rises as the *size* of the holding increases. This progression is not necessary where there is a comprehensive and progressive income tax: the rich would then necessarily get taxed more than the poor. But where, for administrative and other reasons, it is impossible to introduce such a system, the progressive land tax can be a reasonable substitute. In so far as it prompts fragmentation of farms (to reduce the tax liability), this may be consistent with the political aim of creating a rural democracy based on diffused and general ownership of land and with the economic objective of raising productivity through smaller, self-managed farms. On the other hand the fragmentation may be more apparent than real: Indian experience has shown that it is very easy to split up land into below-ceiling or below-high-tax-bracket ranges while keeping it 'in the family'! Since this type of evasion is likely to be self-frustrating in the long run, the success of a progressive land tax is perhaps greater when judged over a longish period.

As for taxes on income and wealth in general, we also need to recall that most underdeveloped countries neglect them appallingly. There is a strong case for shifting to a wider use of the personal income tax, for instance. As of now, many of these countries have not merely a low coverage with exemptions from the tax starting at unduly high income levels but also an ineffective coverage resulting from exemptions granted to several *forms* of income (e.g. agricultural income). From the point of view of both revenue and equity, these omissions have to be repaired. This is especially so in the case of property taxes. The experience of countries such as India suggests that some concentration of wealth is likely to attend the take-off of the underdeveloped areas. This is largely a reflection of the limited availability of entrepreneurial talent in the initial stages of rapid expansion. Inheritance taxes, death duties and wealth levies can help to reduce the adverse economic and political effects of such concentration of wealth, while also yielding some revenue.

A few underdeveloped countries have experimented recently with compulsory savings schemes as a milder alternative to taxation. Turkey, Brazil, Ghana and India are among this small group. The schemes vary a great deal from one country to another. In India, the Compulsory Deposit Scheme applied to income tax assessees alone; the deposits carried interest, were non-negotiable and were repayable at the end of specified periods only. In Ghana, on the other hand, the scheme was linked to the sale of cocoa to a centralised marketing board, 10% of the proceeds being payable in the form of government bonds. It is possible to operate a compulsory savings scheme also by linking it with life insurance or as a form of lottery (as tried out in the form of voluntary 'prize bonds' in India). But whatever form these schemes are given, they suffer from an important limitation. In the long run, it is likely that people will merely switch their voluntary savings to the compulsory category. A Japanese peasant saving normally twenty yen per week and holding it as bank deposit, for example, may merely reduce his bank balance by ten yen and use the withdrawn amount to buy the ten-yen bond which the government forces on him every week: the peasant in this instance has *not* increased, but merely switched, his savings. The net result of compulsory saving schemes may thus be little addition to national resources at great political cost!

These schemes are valuable only when they serve to accustom certain tax-exempt groups to the idea that they *can* be drawn upon to contribute to the nation's resources. For instance, if the government of Nigeria desires to lower the exemption limit so as to bring more people into the income-tax net, it may be politically wise to get these people on to a compulsory savings scheme first, and *then* eventually to put them on the income tax.

In the last analysis, the problem of raising savings through taxation – equitably, efficiently and adequately – belongs to the study of political economy and cannot be divorced from its political setting by an economic analyst. The failure of foreign economic expertise, of a high academic standard, in Ghana and British Guiana in recent experience and the creation in either case of violent political disturbance, remains a sharp reminder of the political realities that constrain the prescription of tax policy in the underdeveloped areas.

13 Investing the resources

Savings and other resources have to be put to a variety of uses. Programmes of expenditure and investment must be formulated, organised and implemented. These decisions have two contrasting aspects: *complementarity* and *competitiveness*. Arising from these, there is a need for an *overall* view of the economy within a planning framework.

The complementarity of programmes and projects is readily understood. If a car has to be produced, a very large number of parts and materials will have to be provided. These in turn will require, for their manufacture, yet other inputs (see figure 23). And so on. The unending chain will certainly be broken at places by imports which eliminate the need for domestic production; but most economies (including several underdeveloped areas) exhibit complex patterns of *input-output*, production processes. These chains can even loop into themselves, reflecting *circularities* in the economic system. This happens, for instance, when steel needs pig iron smelted from iron ore with coking coal which in turn has involved the use of steel (see figure 24).

This pattern of complementarity of economic decisions and processes is to be contrasted with the equally important fact that there are *alternative* ways in which resources may be used to achieve given objectives. Thus, irrigation in an agricultural district may be provided in a centralised fashion by constructing a dam and feeder-channels; alternatively each village in the district may construct a water-tank to catch and store the rains; or each farm may build its well (see figure 25). These different possibilities pose a problem of choice and *not* of complementarity.

These alternatives occur practically everywhere in policy making. For example, if the national objective is to maximise the national income per capita by some target date, the planners may choose from two rival policies. Resources may either be used in promoting population control, through family-planning clinics, bonuses for smaller families, dissemination of information and the subsidisation of contraceptives. Or they may be used to stimulate the growth of incomes directly. Under the former policy, income per capita will

Figure 23. *Complementarity of investment decisions.* This illustration shows the diversity of materials and machinery that have to be made *simultaneously* available if a car is to be manufactured.

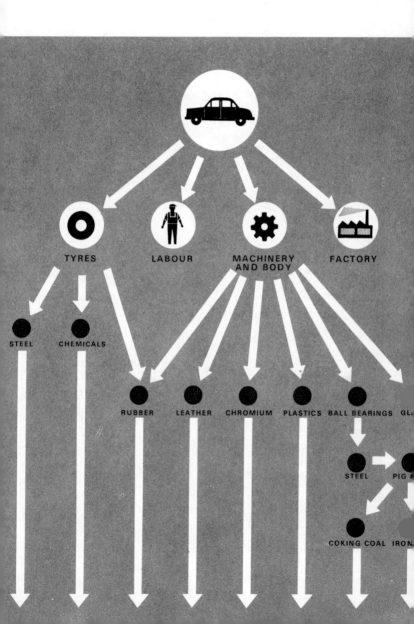

Figure 24. *The interdependence of economic processes which may exhibit circularity.* Steel uses coal which uses, in turn, steel.

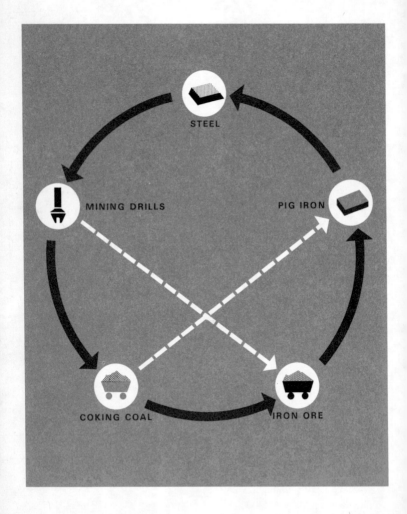

Figure 25. *Investment alternatives*. In a rural area, it may be possible to provide irrigation with a dam *or* wells *or* water-tanks. The investment choice must then be made from all these possibilities if irrigation is to be provided.

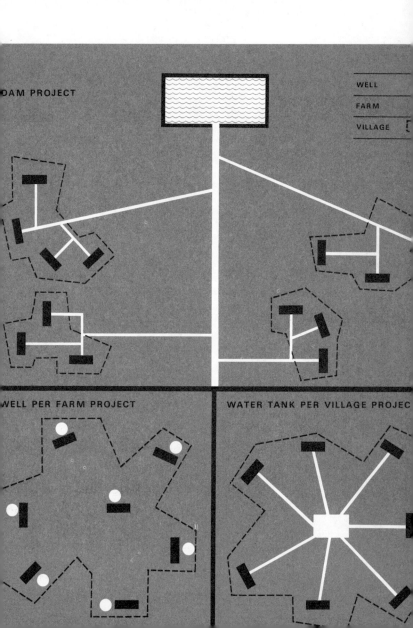

DAM PROJECT

WELL

FARM

VILLAGE

WELL PER FARM PROJECT

WATER TANK PER VILLAGE PROJEC

Figure 26. *Policy alternatives*. Resources may be used to restrict population (Policy I) or to increase income (Policy II).
The choice may be made in terms of the eventual effects of these rival policies on per capita income. In the illustration,
Policy I is superior if the objective is to maximise income per capita at the end of the planning period of fifteen years.

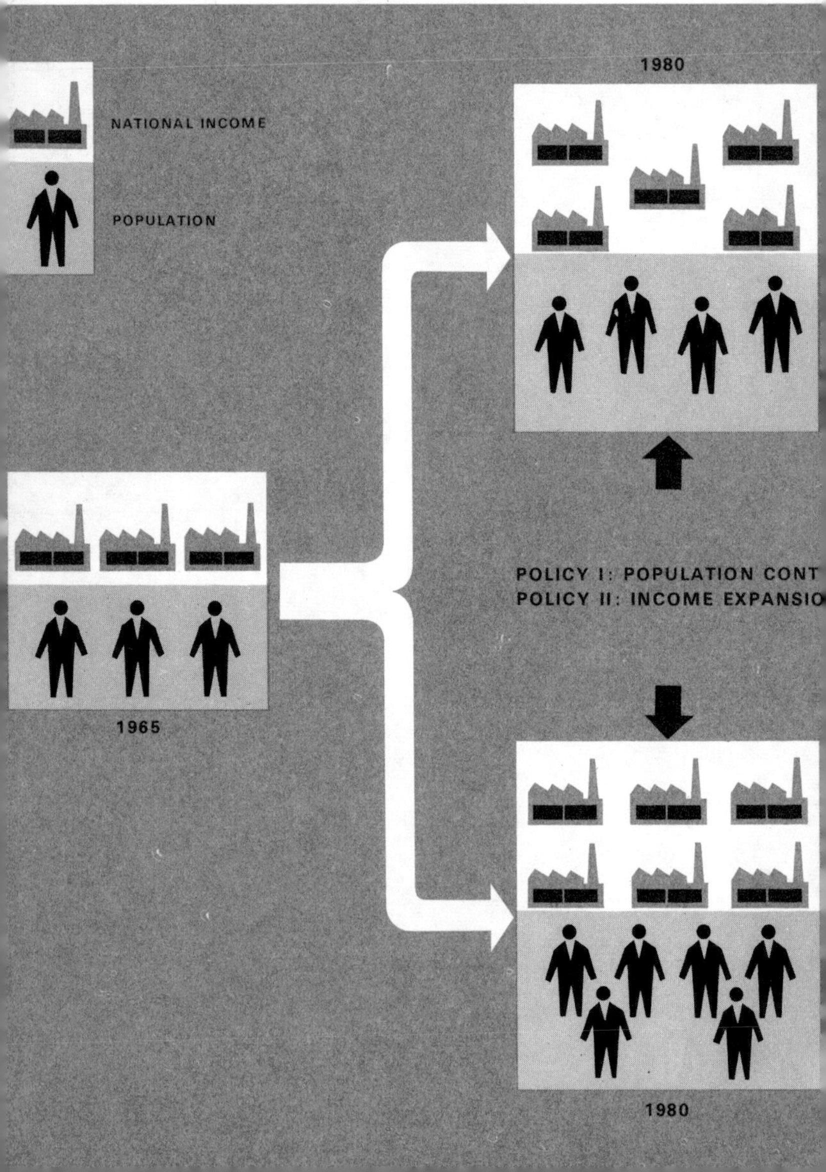

NATIONAL INCOME

POPULATION

1980

POLICY I: POPULATION CONT
POLICY II: INCOME EXPANSIO

1965

1980

rise because of a slowing down of the population growth; under the latter, because of the expansion of income (see figure 26).

In formulating a national programme for achieving any set of objectives, therefore, the authorities must consider both the complementarity and the competitive aspects of their manifold decisions. To do this effectively, a comprehensive view of the available resources and objectives is clearly necessary. The amount to be saved will depend on the total investment proposed; the investment requirement will reflect the income targets; imports will have to be matched with available foreign exchange; the amount of savings to be used for agricultural development will depend on how much is used for industrialisation; and so on. We must, therefore, now proceed to examine in detail the role of a planning framework and the principal aspects of complementarity and competitiveness in plans as typically formulated in many underdeveloped areas today.

14 The planning framework

A good programme will ensure balance on many strategic fronts. Otherwise, crucial shortages and wasteful surpluses will develop as the economy moves ahead. Not that they can be ruled out altogether: no human agency, for example, can foresee weather accurately and be *certain* of agricultural targets; no Planning Commission can take in all the relevant information, with the necessary accuracy; no government can plan on the basis of a totally foreseeable future. And yet this *cannot* be a valid argument for *not attempting* to avoid strategic imbalances – unless it can be forcefully argued, and it cannot, that such attempts would normally accentuate rather than alleviate the imbalances.

Balance is generally sought in four major areas: 1 savings must equal proposed investment; 2 the demand for skilled and unskilled manpower must match its supply in each sector; 3 the availability of commodities and services should be equal to the demand for them; and 4 the import bill must not exceed the available foreign exchange. Let us consider how these balances can be worked out in practice.

1 The matching of savings and investment has already been discussed (in chapter 12). The typical exercise ends up with a table such as table 5, where aggregate savings from different sources equal the aggregate investment – consisting of inventories and fixed capital formation, i.e. machinery and construction generally – in all sectors of the economy.

2 Similarly, it is necessary to match aggregate imports and the available foreign exchange. It is customary to make the calculations so as to fit the format of table 6, where the sum of imports into different sectors and of interest and profit payments equals the earnings of foreign exchange from different exports, *plus* foreign aid and other capital inflow, *plus* the use of foreign exchange reserves which the government may be fortunate enough to possess.

3 Further, the availability of commodities must be equal to the demand for them. Economists generally break this up into four component, balancing exercises: (a) the demand for *consumption* of

130

Table 5. The savings-investment budget for the economy 1965-70 plan

Savings by:		Pesos	Investment in:		Pesos
Domestic	Households	2,100	Fixed	Industry and mining	1,500
	Corporations	200		Agriculture	700
	Central government	300		Services	500
	Local governments	50	Stocks (Inventories)		300
	Public enterprises	30			
Foreign		320			
Total:		3,000	Total:		3,000

Table 6. The foreign exchange budget 1965-70 plan

Available exchange		Pesos	Requirement of exchange		Pesos
Export earnings	Coffee	100	Imports	Machinery	600
	Petroleum	200		Chemicals	200
	Textiles	100		Non-ferrous metals	400
	Tobacco	50		Wheat	150
	Shipping	50		Medical supplies	150
Foreign aid		1,000		Electrical equipment	200
Private capital inflow		200		Locomotives	50
Reserve utilisation		300	Interest on aid		50
			Profit remittances		200
		2,000			2,000

different commodities must equal their availability; (b) the *investment* demand for diverse capital goods, construction materials and inventories must match their supply; (c) the requirements of *intermediate* items (i.e. raw materials) must equal their supply; and (d) planned exports of commodities must be matched by their availability for this purpose.

The consumption exercise is of some significance and needs to be carried out with reasonable accuracy. For example, in India the demand for wheat and rice increases as incomes and population expand. By analysing past behaviour of the demand for these cereals, intelligent guesses can be made of future increases in their consumption under stipulated programmes for increasing national income. These increases have, then, to be provided for through domestic production or imports (plus possible running-down of inventories).

The amount of investment needed has also to be calculated carefully. If 1,000,000 tons of steel is required by 1970 and it is decided to produce it domestically, a steel mill must be constructed. This will call for investment, which is normally computed by observing the *capital-output* ratio in steel production. If the production of one peso-worth of steel requires capital equipment costing on the average three pesos, and if a ton of steel is worth 1,000 pesos, the investment required to produce an annual output of 1,000,000 tons of steel would be 3 billion pesos. This is the figure that must then go into the savings-investment balancing exercise. However, its *physical* counterpart will be blast furnaces, other equipment and construction. These investment *goods* will have to be made available, again through domestic production, imports or the running down of inventories.

The demand for most commodities will also have an intermediate component. Steel, for example, will be used in a wide range of industries. Its demand will thus have to be computed in terms of the production targets of steel-using industries. And so on.

Finally, there will be an export demand for some commodities. If there are plans to export petroleum, for instance, these will have

Table 7. The availability-requirement exercise 1965–70 plan in 1,000 pesos

AVAILABILITY

	Imports	Domestic production	Inventories	Total
Tea	–	90	10	100
Machinery	120	20	–	140
Textiles	100	160	40	300
Wheat	100	70	30	200
Rice	–	90	10	100
Cement	–	900	100	1,000
Steel	1,000	1,200	100	2,300
Petroleum	–	1,400	50	1,450
Electrical equipment	100	–	–	100
Locomotives	50	–	–	50
Medical supplies	400	450	50	900

REQUIREMENT

	Consumption	Capital formation Fixed	Capital formation Inventories	Intermediate	Exports	Total
Tea	30	–	10	–	60	100
Machinery	–	140	–	–	–	140
Textiles	250	–	50	–	–	300
Wheat	160	–	40	–	–	200
Rice	10	–	20	–	70	100
Cement	–	100	160	40	700	1,000
Steel	–	100	100	2,100	–	2,300
Petroleum	400	–	450	100	900	1,450
Electrical equipment	–	100	–	–	–	100
Locomotives	–	50	–	–	–	50
Medical supplies	820	–	80	–	–	900

to be taken into account in fixing the target of petroleum production.

The resulting, *overall* balance is reflected in a table such as table 7, which shows the balancing of availability and requirements (for a hypothetical economy with only eleven commodities). Table 7 presupposes other *supplementary* tables which include, to take two principal examples, one showing that the consumption of each commodity is consistent with the stipulated income and population growth; and another, that the domestic production targets are consistent with the available manpower and capital in these sectors.

Recent advances in computational techniques have made it relatively easy to build up a programme which simultaneously satisfies the different balances we have been discussing so far. Take, for example, the question of balancing requirements and availabilities of different commodities. Since many commodities will be used as intermediates (i.e. raw materials) in other industries, and since there are many circularities in the economic system, how are we to calculate readily the amounts of different commodities that must be produced to satisfy all intermediate demands? If one ton of steel is to be produced, this may need the production of literally dozens of other things which will have to be traced through apparently unending input-output chains. Fortunately the mathematicians have come to the rescue and shown how neat answers can be provided quickly.

The economist is required to set down the *total* demand for commodities in his programme, *exclusive* of intermediate uses: this is often called 'final demand'. This final demand will thus consist of capital formation, addition to inventories, exports (*minus* imports) and consumption; it is also the amount of final demand that *domestic production* must satisfy. If, to this information, the economist can add a 'technical coefficients' table (such as table 8), which shows the quantities of different commodities required to produce each unit of a commodity, the computational technique can readily give the production of each commodity which will be required by way of intermediate inputs to support the assigned programme. With intermediate *and* final demand thus known, the *overall* production level in each sector is determined.

The *full* table that emerges can then be presented as in table 9. It represents a very interesting picture of the *structure* of the economy, laying bare the essential interaction of different sectors of the economic system. The table includes, besides, a large amount of information: on production, imports, exports, intermediate and final demand and national income. It is a representation of the economy which has become very popular recently with planners.

The computational techniques now available are capable of solving such exercises involving several hundreds of sectors of economic activity. However, this is not necessarily an advantage. The possibility of securing information in that amount of detail has not kept pace with the progress of IBM computers. Further, the stability of the technical coefficients often *increases* in practice as the number of sectors is reduced.

Consistency and balance in programmes are thus broadly manageable today. They have, in fact, already been sought by many planners in the underdeveloped areas, most prominently in India and Turkey. Again, one of the most impressive recent developments in Soviet economic science has been the rapid acceptance of modern computational techniques and their ascendancy relative to Marxist dogma and practice. On the other hand, the question of *choice* between alternatives has remained more intractable.

The notion of efficient choice recurs practically throughout the economy. It is necessary to emphasise here the universality of the problem and the corresponding difficulty in tackling it *simultaneously* at all levels. Faced with this difficulty, economists have usually been content to take up certain aspects alone, indulging in what they are fond of describing as 'partial' efficiency (or, in strict jargon, *optimisation*) exercises.

Certain prominent questions are taken up, in such a procedure, and analysed more or less *sequentially*. Thus, as we have already seen, different types of irrigation systems may be compared; or

Table 8. Technical coefficients for the economy 1965–70
Input of items at the left of each row per unit of product listed at the top of each column

	Agriculture and foods	Minerals	Metal fabricating	Fuel and Power	Textiles, leather, and rubber	Transportation (railroad)	All other industries
Agriculture and foods	–	–	–	–	0·0794	–	0·0064
Minerals	0·0066	–	0·0967	0·0014	0·0006	–	0·0092
Metal fabricating	0·0423	0·0183	–	0·0385	0·0169	0·0702	0·0717
Fuel and power	0·0246	0·0749	0·0289	–	0·0197	0·0616	0·0430
Textiles, leather, and rubber	0·0048	–	0·0256	0·0060	–	0·0014	0·0129
Transportation (railroad)	0·0763	0·0919	0·0299	0·1094	0·0024	–	0·0001
All other industries	0·4807	0·3960	0·2736	0·3490	0·4504	0·1680	–

investment in a family-planning campaign may be contrasted with that for expansion of incomes. The choices, when made, would naturally have to be examined for mutual consistency of the types discussed earlier in this chapter. For example, if a programme of birth control is chosen, this would have to be reflected in *reduced* targets for consumption and could well affect the agricultural output targets. This may further affect the choice of irrigation itself: a bigger agricultural target may have justified the construction of a dam whereas a smaller one might not. The complementarity and choice aspects thus *interact*; and planning frequently

Table 9. The structure of the economy 1965–70 in 1,000 pesos

	Agriculture	Mining	Machinery	Other manufacturing	Transport	Other services	Exports	Addition to inventories	Fixed investment	Consumption	Total
Agriculture	10	–	–	200	–	50	100	10	–	400	770
Mining	–	–	·50	20	–	20	40	20	–	50	200
Machinery	–	–	–	–	–	–	30	50	200	–	280
Other manufacturing	80	–	100	10	50	50	30	50	–	200	570
Transport	–	–	20	30	–	–	–	–	–	200	250
Other services	20	10	10	40	30	–	–	–	–	100	210
Imports	10	10	10	30	60	60	–	30	50	40	300
Wages	430	100	60	160	70	20	–	–	–	–	840
Profits and other non-wage incomes	220	80	30	80	40	10	–	–	–	–	460
Total	770	220	280	570	250	210	200	160	250	990	

$$\text{I:} \quad \frac{\text{Total imports}}{300} - \frac{\text{total exports}}{200} = \frac{\text{Foreign aid}}{100}$$

$$\text{II:} \quad \frac{\text{Exports} + \text{addition to inventories} + \text{fixed investment} + \text{consumption}}{200 \qquad 160 \qquad 250 \qquad 990} - \frac{\text{Imports}}{300}$$

$$= \frac{\text{G.N.P.}}{1300} = \frac{\text{Wages} + \text{Profits and other non-wage incomes}}{840 \qquad 460}$$

proceeds in a succession of *interactive* steps of adjustment in diverse decisions.

In later chapters (19–21) we shall discuss some of the principal questions concerning choice which most underdeveloped countries would be well advised to consider. These will necessarily have to be supplemented by other significant analyses of alternatives depending on individual, environmental conditions. At this stage, it is more advantageous to spell out some further aspects of the plan-formulating process. These concern the role of time and space in programme formulation.

15 The time element: phasing and perspectives

So far we have discussed balances and consistency in planning decisions, without bringing time into the calculations in any essential way. The tables of the preceding chapter, for instance, were for the period 1965–70 which symbolised one Five-Year Plan *as a whole*. And yet time enters the planning process significantly. A programme has to be properly *phased*; and there has to be a *perspective* of where the country intends to move in the future.

Phasing and perspectives are essential to a good programme largely, though not entirely, because of the existence of time-lags in decision-making and decision-implementation. Time-lags occur on many fronts: for instance, when a project is being planned. To begin with, there is the question of getting it politically and administratively accepted. In most underdeveloped countries receiving aid this may even involve getting the sanction of the aid-giving country – a process that can be time-consuming and even frustrating. For instance, in trying to get the United States to agree to finance the Bokaro Steel plant in its Fourth Five-Year Plan, the Indian government were faced with protracted negotiations which came to nothing in the end, when the United States government finally declined to provide finance for reasons which were largely buttressed by pressures from *domestic* steel interests. After the sanctioning of a project, the designing stage itself can take up to three years in many industrial projects. Alternative designs pose further questions of choice which take time to settle. And once the project has been designed, investment, management and manpower must be organised. These are time-consuming tasks. Further, a period must elapse before investment results in productive capacity: the erection of a steel mill will take anything up to three years. The attainment of full capacity production is likely to take even longer.

It is possible, therefore, to avoid foreseeable bottlenecks only if projects are planned so as to dovetail neatly into one another. This requires careful phasing of different programmes. If the construction of an irrigation dam is begun in 1966, the *precise* plan for its completion must be laid down. This will enable the planners to

139

know, for instance, how much cement and steel will be required *during each year* of the construction: this will then be reflected in the programmes for cement and steel production. Again, if it is aimed to complete the dam in 1970, the construction of feeder-channels, which will take the water to the farms, must also be programmed so as to synchronise with this target date. Indian planners, in the early years of their work, found that such synchronisation was typically lacking, because few projects had been phased and set out from year to year. The most glaring example of this omission used to be the failure to utilise irrigation waters, not because the farmers were too conservative to respond to the new opportunities, but because there was no way in which the water could be taken to the farms.

It is easy to see that bottlenecks and excess capacity (due to shortage of materials) are likely to be accentuated by unphased or badly phased projects. It is not so obvious that these maladjustments can also lead to balance of payments difficulties. If steel output is not forthcoming at the right time while steel-using industries have already been set up, the demand for steel imports will rise; and (given limited import capacity) the result may be an unmanageable pressure on the balance of payments. This again has happened in India: the Second Five-Year Plan ran into serious balance of payments difficulties largely because of unphased programmes and undue bunching of investments.

Another important implication of the existence of time-lags is that *perspective planning* is necessary if timely decisions are to be taken on projects. If an additional 3,000,000 tons of steel has to be produced in 1975, the question must begin to be discussed around 1968. If the educational system is to turn out 200,000 extra mechanical engineers per annum by 1980, the process of building colleges, and equipping and staffing them, will require decisions by 1970. The future and the present are thus intimately interlocked. A view of the future – sometimes of the quite distant future – is necessary before current decisions can be taken rationally.

Indeed, the future must be worked out in some detail. In the case

The Kariba Dam, on the Zambesi,
which was opened in May 1960.
It took five years to build.

of educational planning, for instance, the number of engineers planned for will reflect the industrial structure envisaged; and so on. For this reason, many developing countries have begun to concede the rationale of having a *Perspective Plan*, which provides the backdrop to, and the guide-lines for, Five-Year and Annual Plans. Indian planners have always had a twenty-five-year period in view, spanning five Five-Year Plans; and since the Second Five-Year Plan, they have formulated ten- and fifteen-year projections for the economy, describing them as perspective plans. The Polish planners have also explicitly formulated a detailed long-term plan. The Turkish state planning organisation has a fifteen-year perspective.

There cannot be any hard and fast rule about the period over which a perspective plan should be formulated. The period must obviously be large enough to cover the biggest time-lags in the system. If educational programmes take the longest to plan and mature, and they take nine years, there would clearly be some sense in taking a perspective view of not less than nine years! But this does *not* rule out the choice of a longer period. The choice must really be arbitrary. The economist, *qua* economist, has nothing to offer in this direction.

A few observations, however, can be made. Firstly, there may be some *strategic* reasons which dictate a specific time-horizon. The Indian planners, for example, chose initially a twenty-five-year perspective because that was the period *during* which they thought they could transform the Indian economy into a position of rapid growth *without foreign aid*. Secondly, it should be recalled that the choice of the time-horizon can affect current economic decisions. Selection from alternative investment policies, for instance, can be sensitive to the length of the planning period (refer back to figure 22).

Another interesting question relating to the time-horizon is whether it should be advanced *annually*. If there is a Five-Year Plan starting in 1960 and ending in 1965, some planners suggest that, in 1961, there should be *another* Five-Year Plan ending in

1966, the time-horizon thus shifting further down as time passes. This is a method practised by Swedish planners and is aptly described as involving '*rolling plans*'. There are technical difficulties in following this procedure. But the real obstacles to it are likely to come from its *political* disadvantages. There is, after all, a great gain in having *steady* targets in terms of which the national effort can be measured and towards which it can be effectively directed; annually changing targets are certain to be very confusing. Political decision-making is also likely to move much more discreetly than annual changes in Five-Year Plans would demand. Perhaps this can be exaggerated: for changes in targets *do* occur in practice, largely because of uncertainty and imperfections in planning methods which result in divergences between performance and plans, calling for adjustment of targets.

Indeed, one of the more significant questions that have recently been raised in relation to the planning process concerns the way in which a plan should be *adjusted* as, with the passage of time, certain assumptions (on which the planners had worked) are seen to be invalid. Suppose that foreign aid turns out to be less than what was planned for. This will inevitably affect the plan. How can the necessary adjustments be best worked out? Or assume that agricultural output has grown less rapidly than allowed for. Should the import-pattern be altered and, if so, how? Experience shows that planners are usually so carried away by the neatness of their exercises that they fail to make due allowance for these probable divergences between plans and actual performance. The result, frequently, is a hasty, indiscriminate slashing of projects which may well be inefficient in view of the national objectives. It is necessary, therefore, to give thought to the principal respects in which the planners' assumptions may be upset and then to work out, *in advance*, the most efficient ways in which adjustments can be made.

16 The space dimension

While the time-element in formulating programmes is thus significant in many ways, so is the space dimension. Practically every country is divided into heterogeneous regions. Many underdeveloped countries, further, have a federal structure, with partial autonomy for the federated states. Ethnically, culturally and politically, therefore, most countries are confronted with pressures for evening out regionally the benefits of their programmes for development. Ethical considerations also reinforce these factors: regional inequalities raise much the same kind of moral questions as other patterns of income and wealth disparities.

Given these political facts, it is amazing how few planning authorities in the underdeveloped areas have given serious attention to the *spatial* (geographical, regional) aspects of their programmes. It is customary – and has been the case except for some outsize and much-publicised projects – to list projects without specifying the areas in which they will come up. Frequently it is actually impossible to get the total investment, revenue and income-expansion targets broken down into regional estimates!

This neglect in plan-formulation has led, in countries such as India, to at least two serious problems which deserve to be discussed at some length.

Firstly, because there are no targeted, guaranteed improvements in the regions (by way of shares in overall national income, employment and investment), the political leaders of individual regions make a scramble for industrial projects every time they are being allocated. This can lead to any or all of the following types of economic inefficiency: 1 A region least suited to support an industry gets it purely because of effective politicking. 2 A project which was just large enough to be economic in its cost of production is split up into three or four smaller projects, each of uneconomic scale and inefficient, so that more than one region can share in the industrial allocation. (It is *not* always wrong, however, to split up projects into uneconomic-scale plants. The geographic distribution of demand, for instance, may be such as to justify having small, *dispersed* plants in different areas, to reduce transport costs. Un-

economic *production* is, in such a case, outweighed by the saving on *transport* costs. But such complications, while they justify uneconomic-size plants sometimes, do *not* justify the political process by which uneconomic-size plants tend to come up most of the time!)
3 In order to weight the allocation towards themselves, the regions may distort economics *elsewhere* so as to make their claims appear more sound. This might happen, for instance, if a region possessing bauxite attempted to get an alumina plant allocated to itself by underpricing electricity to reduce alumina manufacturing costs.

In practice, *all* these patterns of inefficiency are observable in countries without regional plans. In the first fifteen years of Indian planning, for example, these inefficiencies occurred frequently. Production at economic scale was the most serious casualty of the incomplete planning process. This was epitomised in the existence of three automobile plants for producing, between themselves, around 40,000 cars per annum – an average scale of production that was small and cost the nation, unnecessarily, some loss of resources. The widespread nature of uneconomic production in too many plants also hampered the building up of competitive export industries in the field of new manufactures.

The planning framework, on the other hand, could have been adapted to minimise these deleterious results. Technically it should be possible to work out a more efficient allocation of projects and programmes between different regions, *while guaranteeing that no region gets investment and income below certain minimum levels*. The very existence of such a programme would reduce the regional political pressures for *individual* projects by making them less necessary. It is, perhaps, the *uncertainty* of reaching minimum levels of income and investment within the region that makes local leaders keen to grab anything that is 'going'.

The *other* result of neglect of the spatial aspects of planning is to be found on the financial side. If the responsibility for taxation (to increase savings) is not squarely, precisely and quantitatively fixed on local and State governments, the Federal authorities frequently find themselves faced with a serious breakdown in the savings effort. It is not unusual for local and State governments, even when they agree to specific taxation targets, to plead inability later. Such recalcitrance could be remedied, at least to some extent, by making the regional income and investment targets themselves conditional upon fulfilment of the taxation obligations.

We have been discussing, in some detail, the manifold aspects of the planning process, essentially at the level of planning *techniques*. It is necessary now to take up the question from a different angle: from the point of view of the principal sectors of economic activity, agriculture and industry, each in turn.

17 Revolution in agriculture

Many analysts tend to underestimate the importance of improving the agricultural sector in developing economies. This is because they stress the role of industrialisation. But the two need not be in conflict. Agriculture and industry compete, of course, for national resources. But this does *not* mean that those who emphasise the need for agricultural expansion should necessarily be opposed to industrialisation.

Agricultural transformation is important for a variety of reasons, any or all of which may be relevant to a specific underdeveloped country. Take, for instance, the sheer size of this sector in the underdeveloped countries. If the non-agricultural sector grew at a rate of 10% and the agricultural sector at a rate of 2% in an underdeveloped country with 80% G.N.P. in agriculture, the country's overall growth rate would be only $3\cdot6\%$. A high rate of expansion in the underdeveloped countries is thus impossible unless this massive sector is prodded into rapid transformation.

But it is not just this arithmetic that makes agriculture so important. There are many links between agriculture and other sectors of the economy which make agricultural expansion equally vital. Industrial expansion itself depends on agriculture in several major respects. Agricultural raw materials enter many industries: cotton textiles use raw cotton, groundnut oil needs oilseeds; and so on. Nearly one-third of India's industrial output recently depended upon the supply of agricultural commodities such as raw cotton, jute, oilseeds and rice.

Less obvious, but of equal significance, is the role played by the availability of food supply in industrialisation. As we have previously seen (chapter 12), workers usually cannot be absorbed in industrial activity unless they are fed by the countryside. The ruthless collectivisation of Soviet agriculture was forced by the failure of the kulaks to market enough foodstuffs, combined with the lack of sufficient foreign exchange to enable supplies to be increased by imports.

In countries where the amount of labour available is limited, the transformation of agriculture also has an important role to play in

Farmers of the Muntilan Fish Culture Centre in Central Java putting fingerlings in the wet paddy field. By the time the rice is ripe the fish will have grown to five or six inches. Fisheries officers from many South East Asian countries have gone to Java to learn about paddy fishery.

providing industrial labour. Greater productivity per man in agriculture makes it possible to release labour for non-agricultural occupations.

In countries where the agricultural population, on the other hand, outstrips the number of jobs on the land and its rate of growth is large, the need for rapid agricultural transformation can be equally acute. The need springs in this case, among other reasons, from the necessity to prevent an overflow of population to the cities, in a futile search for employment.

Historically, agriculture has also been observed to accelerate growth by earning valuable foreign exchange. The post-Meiji industrialisation of Japan, for example, was crucially assisted by rapidly expanding agricultural exports.

These economic arguments are accentuated, in most underdeveloped countries, by the political significance of *rural* development (which must inevitably be founded on a prosperous agriculture). The governments of these countries have begun to appreciate the *naïveté* of expecting the rural masses to identify themselves with national programmes, and with the authorities, if they do not take these programmes to the countryside. The politicians cannot afford to forget that more than three-quarters of their electorate lives in the rural areas.

The programme for agricultural transformation, while one of the most crucial, is also the most complex to think through and carry out. In many developing countries, efforts at agricultural progress have failed because of inadequate attention to one or more of the many components of a successful policy. This has resulted in frustration, waste of limited resources and halting progress in other, complementary activities. The recent, agonising focus on agriculture by the Soviet Union and Communist China is eloquent testimony to the limitations of ill-conceived programmes in the field of agriculture.

An effective agricultural policy requires *simultaneous* action on three principal fronts. 1 Because of the primitive nature of techniques in use on the land, provision must be made for the effective

transmission of new techniques to the farmers. This is a matter of supplying the *knowledge*: an activity which is now commonly known as 'extension service'. 2 Further, steps must be taken to make the farmers *willing* to adopt these new techniques. This is a question of creating the conditions which will provide sufficient incentives and inducements to farmers to invest in progress. These conditions relate chiefly to marketing facilities, price expectations and the system of land tenure (whose effect on the farmer's ability to reap the reward of his efforts is of great significance). 3 Finally, it is necessary to ensure that the implementation of new techniques by willing farmers is not frustrated through lack of inputs and finance. Water, fertilisers, and better seeds must be supplied on time. And the farmers must be given the necessary credit facilities so that they can make the required investments. This *supply* aspect is so clearly necessary to a coherent programme that it is surprising how often it is ignored in the developing countries.

We must discuss these three aspects in some detail. It will be useful, however, to begin by looking at them from the point of view of developing countries whose political persuasions rule out the institution of *collectivisation* – whether of the Soviet or of the more ambitious, Chinese communes, variety. We shall assume initially that the problem of agricultural transformation has to be looked at as one which involves the handling of a vast mass of farmers, with private ownership (of varying forms) in land. Only later shall we touch upon the question of collectivisation; this will be necessary, despite the disrepute into which the method seems to have fallen, because there are some interesting lessons to be learnt from it.

Provision of knowledge: extension service

The discrepancy between traditional practices in the agricultures of the developing countries and modern processes shows that rapid strides in agricultural progress can be made. A pre-condition of this progress, however, is the dissemination of knowledge to thousands (and sometimes hundreds of thousands) of individual, scattered farmers.

Experience shows that this task is an enormously difficult one. And the difficulties arise *not* merely because, as extension workers are only too eager to claim, the farmers are conservative and unwilling to learn and innovate. They are due mainly to the fact that farmers tend to be shrewd and realistic in their evaluation of the new ideas being handed out by government officials. Given the risks involved in hasty application of what appear to him as half-baked ideas, the farmer naturally wants to make sure that experiments are not undertaken at his expense. The role of demonstration farms is therefore very important. They are also an important check on the utility of the techniques being recommended by extension workers. It is useful to recall the early experience of Japan in this respect. The Japanese initially imported Western techniques somewhat indiscriminately. These techniques suited the larger Western farms and were brought back by Japanese officials visiting America and England in the late nineteenth century. But they rapidly had to be abandoned and replaced by techniques more suited to Japanese conditions of farm size, weather and soil.

The demonstration farms must, furthermore, be close to the villagers. It is insufficient to have such farms in remote areas, or closer to the towns where the bureaucracy is likely to be located. These farms should really be in every village covered by an extension service. An added argument for this view is that soil and other factors sometimes vary widely from village to village, making it necessary for techniques to be adapted to individual circumstances.

An intensive approach, with demonstration farms for every village, needs to be supplemented by well-paid, trained workers in the extension service. Indian experience shows that burdening 'village-level workers' with all kinds of duties, and recruiting fairly low-calibre staff because of small salaries can easily cause an extension service programme to fail. This kind of waste of resources results from a desire to spread the extension programme widely with limited funds.

But it is not enough merely to have well-trained and intelligent village-level workers. It would be enough, and in fact was so, in countries such as the United States where the farmers themselves have traditionally been eager to learn new techniques and have high levels of literacy. But in the traditional societies of the developing countries, the extension worker has to go much further and *evoke* a response. And here it is wise to appreciate the limitations of human nature. Village-level workers with fixed salaries and security of service are unlikely, except in rare cases of idealism and dedication, to put in the required effort. There is a clear case here for building in an economic incentive for the extension worker. It has been proposed, in the Indian context, that it would be useful to have part of the village-level worker's salary related, as with salesmen, to the rate at which new techniques are being adopted in his village. This could be done for example by relating the commission to the sales of fertilisers, new seeds and so on. In fact, it may even be possible to generalise this scheme and relate the commission to the growth of output itself in the village. This would give the

Students at work at one of Nigeria's farm
institutes set up by the government in association
with FAO. More than 80% of the 35,000,000 people
in Nigeria are employed in agriculture, which
not only produces the country's food but
accounts for 90% of its export trade.

village-level worker an interest in promoting even those techniques
and investments (such as drainage, crop-rotation, terracing and
bunding) which are not related to new inputs like fertilisers but
which, none the less, contribute to agricultural progress. These
schemes are naturally attractive to economists; but there is likely
to be considerable difficulty in introducing such practical ideas
into a field dominated by misguided reliance on idealistic methods.

The role of literacy must also be stressed in this context. In
Japan again, a significant contribution seems to have been made by
the many educational facilities available to literate farmers,
enabling them to pick up technical knowledge. 'Technical supplementary schools' were expanded rapidly in Japan and in these
agriculture was frequently stressed. Where standards of literacy
have been raised, this Japanese method could be tried successfully.

Willingness to invest and innovate

Even when persuaded that it is possible to raise yields by the application of new techniques, the farmer must not be expected to adopt
these techniques immediately. Perhaps the most important factor
determining his decision to invest in new techniques will be the
reward that he expects from them. This factor is intimately linked
with the land tenure system and with the kind of markets and
prices he expects for his output.

There are so many varieties of land tenure in the underdeveloped
countries that it would be tedious to discuss them all. Nor is it
necessary to do so. All that we need emphasise is the utter im-
probability of a farmer carrying out investments if his return is
slashed because he has to share the results of his efforts with his
landlord. No one is less likely to be a progressive farmer than a
rack-rented tenant. In some states in India, the proportions of
extra output that had to be handed over to the landlord used to be
as high as three-quarters. Land reform, to rule out these practices,
is absolutely essential if progress is to take root firmly in agriculture.
How far such reform can be effective is, however, another matter.

It is easy enough to put legislation on the statute books. But the actual implementation can be extremely difficult. Instances are known where the apparent share of the landlord is reduced but the real share remains at the previous, exorbitant level. Redress against such evasion of legislation is difficult for a variety of reasons. Litigation, for example, is time-consuming and expensive. The landlord belongs to the Establishment and an ordinary tenant is unlikely to expect redress either from the bureaucracy or from the judiciary, both of which he is likely to identify with the landlord class. And so, unless the structure of political power in the villages is strikingly altered, it is naïve to expect far-reaching land reforms to take firm root in the rural economy.

This sad conclusion is unfortunately applicable also to land reform which is aimed at creating ownership in land in preference to cultivation on a tenancy basis. The creation of a rural democracy, based on general ownership of land, is for many an objective in itself. However, there are economic arguments which support it. Perhaps the most fundamental is that based on incentives. A farmer who tills his own land is likely to put in his best efforts because the return will accrue entirely to him. The investments in bettering the farm will also belong to him, whereas if he were only a tenant they would accrue to the landlord.

On the other hand, while most economists would be willing to concede the case for converting tenants into owners, through land-reform legislation, there is not likely to be such consensus on the question of breaking up large farms (employing hired labour) into smaller farms owned by a wider number of people. Before we discuss the merits of such a policy, however, let us consider how this reform may be effected. The simplest way is to legislate a ceiling on farm size. Alternatively, a progressive tax, assessed on farm size, would encourage a break-up of large farms with heavier tax liability. This type of land reform, however, is among the most difficult to implement. It is very easy to have a nominal break-up of land in an extended family, with brothers dividing up the property among themselves for example. But, assuming that the land reform can be carried through, would it be economically desirable?

There are many analysts who feel that the resulting pattern of small farms would be economically inefficient. According to them, large farms would be more responsive to technical progress and would reduce considerably the costs of transmission of knowledge and materials to the rural areas. Small plots, on the other hand, would make economic cultivation difficult (as, for example, when a tractor is impossible for a small man to own and use fully on his farm). Offsetting these arguments, however, is the fact that in countries such as India small farms have been observed to turn out greater output per acre. And the reasons may well be the greater incentive to work on the part of the tiller and the prevalence of the peasant family system on these small farms. The latter enables the owner-farmer to exploit his land fully whereas, on the larger farms with hired labour, production is carried only so far as it will cover the hiring charges. (This can be seen in figure 27. ABC

Figure 27. *Loss of production when surplus labour is available only at a wage.*
A B C represents incremental output as labour is *increased* on the farm.
(At point O, some labour is *already* employed and the incremental output from
the last labourer is O A.) With wage-rate O W, a farmer will
hire labour up to O D. Additional labour will cost him
more than its contribution to increasing output. So B C D measures the
loss of output if additional labour is available but only at wage O W.

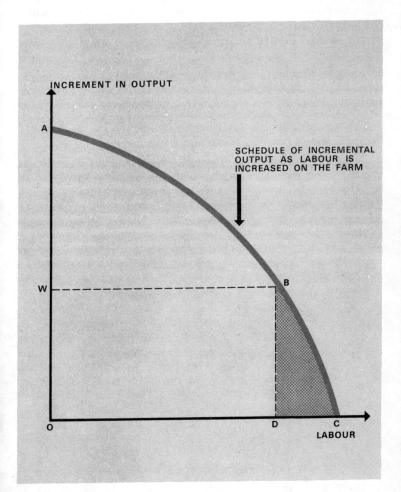

INCREMENT IN OUTPUT

A

SCHEDULE OF INCREMENTAL
OUTPUT AS LABOUR IS
INCREASED ON THE FARM

W · · · · · · · · · · · · · · · B

O   D   C
                          LABOUR

Indian farmers examining a new strain of
wheat at a research farm in Delhi.
The farm, which is an integral part
of the extension services,
invites farmers twice a year to
inspect its results.

represents the schedule of *incremental* output from a farm as more
and more labour is put to work on a given piece of land. The schedule shows diminishing returns as more labour is employed. Where
the labour is hired at wage-rate OW, it will not pay the farmer to
employ labour beyond the point D because the wage will exceed
the extra output that additional labour will produce. On the other
hand, a peasant family will carry output right up to the point C.
Thus the shaded area BCD will represent the extra output that a
peasant family system will produce in contrast to the system in
which labour hired at wage-rate OW is used.)

These reasons can be quite significant and may make the small
farm efficient in practice. It can also be argued that the economies
of marketing, supply of knowledge and so on can be effectively

simulated, in a small-farm system, by the institution of *co-operative societies* designed for this purpose. And even indivisible pieces of equipment, such as tractors, can be made available easily and efficiently by *centralising* the supply in a pool and letting out equipment to individual farmers on hire.

The problems of marketing facilities and price expectations are as important as those concerning land reform. A farmer is unlikely to have much incentive to go in for fresh investments if he is not sure of the return that he will get from his market sales. Indeed, marketing facilities may not be available at all. In many developing countries, a network of markets, linking the expected growth in agricultural supplies with the rising towns and cities, will be an essential part of the process of agricultural transformation. The role of co-operative marketing in these countries hardly needs to be stressed. It would both provide marketing facilities and secure for the farmers the large profit-margins which otherwise accrue to middlemen. In Denmark and Japan, to take two outstanding examples, co-operatives have played a significant role in providing marketing facilities and reasonable prices to the member-farmers. But these societies are the creation of the farmers themselves. In the developing countries, the bulk of the work in starting them will have to be done by the governments. And here there are possibilities of failure. Co-operative societies imposed from outside take time to acquire roots. Inducements provided to co-operate societies, through cheap credit and other assistance, may also lead – as they often have in India – to the creation of dummy societies which have little to do with the stated purposes. These caveats need to be fully appreciated before embarking on a programme of support for the co-operative marketing movement in the developing countries.

Supplementing the organisational facilities for marketing, there is need for a policy of price stabilisation in agriculture. If there is *instability* in the prices that the farmer expects, it can be disastrous to him in undertaking new investments. A farmer borrowing and investing 5,000 yen, who is expected to pay interest at 10% and repay 1,000 yen at the end of the first year, will be faced with disaster

if he is not sure of the price at which he can sell the year's output. It is just not enough to point out to him that he will break even over a long period; he does not have, in the majority of cases, the staying power that this argument assumes. It is for this reason that economists have recommended that the market prices which the farmer gets should be stabilised. The rationale of such a scheme is so obvious that politicians everywhere have readily agreed to it. But these schemes have rarely been implemented in practice. In India, for instance, despite a wide consensus, they have been adopted only sporadically and with inadequate coverage.

One of the serious limitations in the field of incentives for farmers is the indebtedness which many of them seem to inherit or acquire. This frequently means that the bulk of any rise in income has to be handed over to the moneylender. On the other hand, it is possible to argue that the threat of bankruptcy and possible loss of tenancy or land, inherent in a situation of heavy indebtedness, may prompt larger efforts from the subsistence farmers. The question is ticklish, but economists have generally inclined towards the thesis that rural indebtedness is an unmitigated disaster from the economic point of view and that measures ought to be taken to reduce it, through legislation.

A Peruvian farmer controlling an irrigation canal high up in
the Andes mountains. This irrigation scheme, which is financed
by the United States, is not completely efficient since the
force of the water tends to erode the top soil. But it is better
than no irrigation at all and has helped to grow more wheat.
The farms are very poor and cheap methods are essential.

Supply of materials and finance

One of the crucial elements in the programme will have to be
the availability of finance for the farmer. In most Asian, Middle
Eastern and some Latin American countries the farmers are at the
mercy of local moneylenders, who cannot be regarded as either
adequate or desirable sources of credit for investment-minded
farmers. This situation in many underdeveloped countries can be
remedied by the creation of banks and co-operative credit societies
in the rural areas. This is the policy pursued by the Indian authorities. But it is worth recording some of the unforeseen difficulties
that the Indian efforts have encountered. Since financial security
has been demanded to back loans, the credit given by these institutions has tended to by-pass the small but needy farmers. Loans
have also tended to be made to creditworthy landowners and
moneylenders who, having borrowed at cheap rates, have re-lent
to others at the traditionally high rates *and* for non-agricultural
purposes, so that the objectives of the rural credit programme have
often been frustrated. Methods of avoiding such pitfalls will have
to be devised, suited to specific contexts.

The availability of irrigation, fertilisers, pesticides, equipment,
better livestock and better seeds is a relatively easier problem for
planners. And yet it needs to be carefully planned. Instances are
known where the superintendents of irrigation canals fail to give
sufficient notice of their intention to close down a canal for reasons
such as shortage of water. Such inefficient procedures can ruin
crops and do incalculable damage to an extension programme.
There are also numerous examples of field channels not having
been put down for long periods, so that the irrigation water could
not be used at all. Frequently irrigation water is spread too thinly
over a wide area and returns from irrigation are correspondingly
diminished. In the case of fertilisers again, there is need to make the
supplies available on time and in the right amounts. The co-
ordination of the supply of different inputs also needs to be appreciated. Most chemical fertilisers, for example, need additional

water. If they are used without it, they not merely fail to raise productivity but may even reduce it.

Package programme

What is required is a proper co-ordination of all these elements of a successful agricultural programme. Having noted that an un-co-ordinated and thinly spread programme of agricultural progress had failed to generate sufficient momentum, the Indian government have now adopted the so-called 'package programme'. The intention here is to *concentrate* on a few districts and to go all out in giving them an *integrated* programme for expansion.

Added to the need for thoroughness and concentration in order to avoid an ineffective spread of resources, there is need for a pragmatic and *flexible* evaluation and adaptation of agricultural policies. More so than practically any other sector, agriculture invites the enthusiasm and idealism of far too many uninformed and doctrinaire analysts. The success of the Japanese agricultural revolution in the post-Meiji era has been attributed chiefly to the flexibility of the planning methods. For instance, the 1900 Act which established agricultural co-operatives was continuously revised in the light of experience. So were the price-stabilisation policies carried out by the government.

Other questions

Certain other, broader aspects of a rural programme have recently received attention. One is the role that *other* rural measures have to play in the process of agricultural transformation. An influential school of thought emphasises the need to integrate the measures for agricultural expansion (such as a package programme) with a rural programme of health, sanitation, education and welfare activities. This has been the approach underlying the Community Development Programme of the Indian government, for example. The idea seems attractive. But time and again these projects have been seen to divert too many funds and resources to non-agricultural activities. Poor yields and less food have been in striking contrast to the steel slides and community centres in the villages covered by some of these projects. To those who seek rapid increases in agricultural output, the priority implicit in this approach is unacceptable. No doubt over a long stretch of time, these activities will create favourable conditions for greater productivity. But in most developing countries the perspective this argument demands is too distant from the pressing needs of the next ten to fifteen years. Therefore, while integrated community development is desirable *in itself*, one must be realistic and admit that it is likely to have little relation to agricultural productivity except over a very long time-span.

Another significant question concerns the role that small industries and urbanisation can play in assisting agricultural transformation. In modern Japan, as also in the prosperous and progressive agricultural areas of India (such as the Punjab), rapid agricultural progress has been associated with the growth of small industries and urban centres. This has led some analysts to postulate a causal relationship between these phenomena. But it is equally likely that they are both the results of the initiative of an energetic and investment-minded population. This is an interesting but debatable issue; and we shall have occasion to refer to it again (in chapter 20) when we analyse the case for small industries.

Voluntary labour

Finally, we must touch on two other questions of interest: 1 the role of voluntary labour; and 2 collectivisation. In areas with surplus labour, governments are tempted to exhort villagers to *donate* labour for jobs such as road-building, construction of schools and other communal activities. This idea is attractive, provided it works (see chapter 6). But it does not work too well – if experience in countries such as India is any guide. The failure stems not merely from lack of enthusiasm for community-work. Rather it stems from the conflict of class interests, as highlighted by the refusal of a landless labourer to participate in voluntary road construction on the ground that: 'It will merely enable the rich farmers to bring their cars from the town into the village. How will it help me?' Those who profit most from such activities are those who are least likely to contribute manual labour; and those who profit least, and frequently not at all, are usually the only people who will do manual work.

To get over these difficulties, a poll tax has been suggested which can be paid in terms of labour-hours or money. The poorer and underemployed sections will naturally pay in terms of labour-hours. This system is traceable to levies in medieval Europe (such as the *corvée*) which appear to have worked efficiently. Practically no underdeveloped country, however, appears to have tried it so far. And yet it deserves more attention than it has received. Supplementing the package-programme approach, this method of utilising surplus labour, if carefully organised, can have much larger coverage and lead to a considerable addition to national wealth at little cost.

Collectivisation

The institution of collectivisation, and its more extreme form of the Chinese communes, has often been advocated as a panacea for the agricultural sector. At the same time, it is considered by many to have failed the test of actual experimentation. The cause of this failure appears to be that the authorities have relied on effort by individual members without providing adequate incentives for individual betterment. This lack of incentives is supposed to have jeopardised the productivity of collective farms by sapping the mainsprings of sustained effort. While many would argue that no incentive system on a collective farm can match the incentive inherent in the cultivator's ownership of his land, there is no reason to believe that the Soviet-type collectives cannot be prompted into greater productivity by a more judicious and generous use

A ten-mile village road connecting the
village of Bannigiri in India's Mysore State to the
main highway was built with a voluntary
grant of land plus voluntary labour.
Before this the village was literally cut
off from the outside world.

of incentive schemes. The introduction of private holdings by collective farmers (however small) and various backdoor methods of introducing the profit motive in Soviet farming, which Mr Krushchev has recently publicised, hold out the promise of greater efficiency in Soviet agriculture.

The Chinese experiment is more difficult to assess in view of the limited and biased information that is available. While the communes are regarded generally as failures, there is a divergent view that they actually helped the Chinese government to tide over the effects of bad harvests and floods with smaller economic and social hardships than in the more anarchistic, pre-commune days. It is too early to reach a judgment on them. But, it can be argued that, with China's teeming millions (in contrast to the Soviet situation), the commune approach is likely to represent an efficient (though *not* the only efficient) way of organising agriculture. Where so many men are available, it does not really matter that they do not work with maximum efficiency! Moreover, by *de facto* working on the principle of a peasant family system, the communes are likely to be more productive than alternative arrangements based on a hired labour system (as seen in figure 27).

Possibility of rapid growth

What are the prospects for rapid growth of agricultural output? It is customary for most extension officials to be defeatist on this issue. A growth rate of 3–4% is regarded as quite optimistic. An average performance of 2–3% is considered eminently reasonable. With agriculture so predominant a part of national income in many developing countries, this view condemns most of these countries to an unduly low rate of income growth. But this pessimism is really unfounded. Even the Indian performance over the first decade of planning during 1950–60 has been 3·5%. And the recent phenomenal success of Yugoslavia in raising agricultural output by over 50% in under a decade is a stimulating reminder of what can be achieved by a concerted and sustained effort.

18 Industrialisation

The issue of industrialising the underdeveloped countries easily arouses passions. The opposition to industrialisation tends to be as doctrinaire and unyielding as its advocacy.

Conservative political opinion usually inclines towards a view of the world economy in which the poor countries specialise in primary production and import their requirements of manufactures from the richer nations. This picture is rationalised by persuasive appeals to economic doctrines (such as the principle of division of labour) whose real implications are not understood at all. The radical proponents of industrialisation equally seem to be content to cite spurious arguments to support a pre-conceived conclusion.

But the debate can easily be raised to an intellectually respectable and profitable level. In fact, a large number of arguments can be used to defend a policy of industrialisation. Not all of them are totally persuasive; but some are quite impressive. The most compelling perhaps is that industrialisation is a simple consequence, for most developing countries, of inadequately expanding exports. It is possible to argue that poor countries should continue producing primary products *only* if it can be established that they could always earn enough foreign exchange to import their manufactures. Where this is not so, industrialisation is a *rational* consequence. And this *is* the case for many developing countries.

But there are also other, supplementary factors that appear to make industrialisation desirable. It has been claimed for example that industrialisation brings in its wake inventiveness, a modern outlook, the environment for rapid technological progress, indeed the whole complex of industrial civilisation which is necessary for a progressive nation. These advantages do not seem to obtain in non-industrialised countries. And the fact that Belgium, Denmark and Australia have large agricultural sectors and are yet technologically advanced and inventive is *not* a contradiction, because they have quite large manufacturing sectors as well. Obviously these sociological arguments are not decisive: but to many analysts, the empirical evidence seems highly suggestive and even a satisfactory basis for the policy of industrialisation.

The Karabuk steelworks in Turkey.
With the establishment of a
second works at Eregli, the
Turkish government aims to increase
per capita output of steel sixfold
in a decade.

Again, the fairly strong empirical association of industrialisation and high national incomes (as in figure 9) is often considered conclusive. But clearly, as with the sociological arguments, this association cannot really be treated as definitive.

In practice, these propositions are reinforced by strictly political considerations (which can, of course, be quite important from the point of view of overall, national objectives). Thus, for example, even if a country can conceivably continue as a primary producer and rely on trade for imports of manufactured consumer and capital goods, it may prefer not to do so. And this decision may be motivated by considerations of security – greater reliance on foreign sources for capital goods, for example, may jeopardise investment plans during a political crisis. This may be tantamount in a specific case to overrating the risks of non-industrialisation; but then it is the assessment which is false in this case and *not* the form of argument, which is quite valid.

Thus economic, sociological and political factors may reinforce one another in making industrialisation a desirable policy for developing countries. Of course this does not rule out the possibility that some underdeveloped country may find it profitable to adhere to specialisation in primary production. But it does mean that any *a priori* condemnation of industrialisation by the developing countries is based on ignorance or doctrinaire arguments. And this is precisely why the industrialisation policies of these countries have now come to be accepted more readily.

The role of heavy industry

Although most economists concede that industrialisation in the developing countries could be desirable, they often fail to see any rationale in the development of *heavy industry*. The erection of steel and capital-goods plants is looked upon as indulgence in 'conspicuous consumption' by wasteful governments and dismissed as tantamount to economic inefficiency.

This view rests on the preconception, derived from outmoded

economic thinking, that heavy industry is capital-intensive and hence should not be attempted by capital-scarce, underdeveloped countries. But it ignores some important, empirical reasons which make the development of heavy industry not merely necessary in some developing countries but also less expensive than might be imagined.

The principal reason to be noted is the one we have already cited earlier when developing the case for industrialisation in general: namely, the limitation imposed by stagnant or inadequate export earnings. Take the case of an underdeveloped country, relying on exports of primary products and faced with little prospect of being able to increase earnings of foreign exchange from these exports. Assume that in 1970, this country expects to have $100 million by way of foreign exchange (through earnings and capital inflow). Assume also that, in 1970, it wants to be able to invest, in plant and equipment (e.g. tractors, fertiliser factories, dam-building machinery, etc.) $250 million. This proposed investment, however, cannot be met by imports alone. $150 million of required plant and equipment cannot be imported in 1970. The country must therefore plan to *produce* for itself the $150 million-worth of plant and equipment. The development of heavy industry is thus, for countries such as this – and they may be typical – a direct outcome of the limited availability of foreign exchange in relation to their import requirements. And it is a perfectly legitimate and sensible phenomenon.

It would undoubtedly be an expensive method of growth. The country may not possess adequate raw materials. The necessary skills may not be readily available. But this merely means that an increased rate of investment and growth in this country is correspondingly more difficult and exacting. It does *not* mean that an easier solution is available – for it is not, given the foreign exchange bottleneck.

In point of fact, a country such as India, which has had to go in for heavy industry largely for these reasons, has found her progress greatly helped by two fortuitous circumstances. First, she has abundant coal and iron ore deposits, which are among those of the best quality in the world. Secondly, she has had access to technical assistance in this field initially from the Soviet Union but increasingly from other industrially advanced countries as well. This has made the task of constructing and operating these complex enterprises manageable.

These sound, economic arguments make the case for heavy industry unassailable in the developing countries to which they are applicable. However, a good case can be spoilt by a bad advocate. And this has tended to happen here, thanks to certain specious arguments which have gained circulation at the hands of some planners. For example, it is sometimes argued that a domestic steel industry is necessary to higher growth because there is a positive association between steel consumption and gross national product. Needless to say, the proposition is a *non sequitur*. Only when combined with some additional assumption, such as an exchange bottleneck, does the argument begin to look intellectually respectable.

But even when a policy of industrialisation has been adopted, and the industrial programme dovetailed into the overall planning framework (as described in chapter 14), a large number of questions remain to be answered. For example, how much of the proposed programme should be assigned to the public (governmental) sector? How can efficiency be achieved in public enterprises? Are there dangers that economic power will be unduly concentrated in the private sector, and can governmental policy avoid this? Is the creation of an industrial labour force likely to pose difficulties? What degree of controls and detailed planning is efficient? These and other *operational* questions are vital. Policies aimed at resolving them efficiently need to be devised and carried out.

Public sector v. private sector

The economic case for public-sector participation in industrial activity rests on the premises that 1 an activity may be socially profitable but not privately remunerative; and 2 it may be privately profitable but, for some reason, not capable of private execution.

The former reason explains the entry of the government into what are called 'social overhead capital' areas. Roads and ports are excellent examples: their many benefits are not entirely recoverable by private investors (even if toll charges could be levied, as they cannot always be). But the argument really extends beyond these overhead facilities.

In rapidly expanding, underdeveloped countries, growth can involve striking changes in the structure of production. These

Heavy industry in India.
At a factory in Parambur the
sides of a coach are being
rolled into position
with the help of the
overhead crane.

changes can hardly be anticipated by decentralised, atomistic entrepreneurs. This has happened, for instance, in the case of the Indian steel industry. The planners invariably set higher targets of steel output than the private entrepreneurs thought appropriate. This was natural, as private expectations were based on the *past* performance of the economy and did not take sufficient account of the coming changes in the industrial structure. As events turned out, the steel targets were inadequate even in relation to needs.

Clearly, therefore, the State needs to intervene, through public-sector investments, in those industries about which private expectations are ill-informed and inadequate. (And these industries usually tend to be capital-goods rather than consumer-goods industries. This is largely explained by the fact that capital-goods industries need a longer perspective and hence are more susceptible to the kind of distortions discussed here.)

It may be, and indeed has been, argued that public-sector investment is unnecessary and that the dissemination of 'correct' information about future projections would be sufficient to induce the desired investment by private entrepreneurs. This argument, however, is easily refutable: mere information need not necessarily lead private entrepreneurs to change their expectations.

Supplementing these arguments for the entry of the public sector into industrial programmes is the fact that some of the investments may be beyond the ability of individual entrepreneurs to organise. Or (more likely) their cost may be well over the financial resources that can be raised from the available financial institutions. This is likely to be so again with respect to capital-goods projects, which can be large and can use a large amount of capital. It may be contended, however, that this does not necessarily establish the case for public-sector investment. For instance, the government could itself supply the necessary finance to private entrepreneurs or improve existing financial markets. True, but the choice between these different alternatives is not a matter purely of ideology. The choice in favour of public-sector investment is likely to be dictated also by the tardy and uncertain nature of the other alternatives.

However, these economic arguments frequently buttress the *political* objective of creating a larger public sector. This, for example, is the declared objective of the Indian government, the underlying aim being the ultimate creation of a preponderant governmental ownership of the means of production. With a steadily rising proportion of investment going into the public sector in every Plan, the eventual dwarfing of private-sector ownership of capital is certain. A *gradualist* approach to the Marxist goal is thus implicit in this policy. The expansion of the public sector may, however, sometimes be the result of extraneous considerations rather than of political convictions. Thus, for example, it is important to remember that the United States prefers to channel its aid into the private sector whereas the Soviet Union and other socialist countries overwhelmingly finance public-sector projects. A country receiving aid, especially when it has no strong ideological convictions one way or the other, is likely to adjust its economic organisation to the aid donor's preferences.

Efficiency in public enterprises

It is frequently debated whether public-sector projects will be efficiently run. There is undoubtedly a tendency in many countries to run these enterprises like government departments – with all the attendant red-tape, bureaucratic indecision and soft-pedalling. And the resulting atrophy and unimaginative operation are immune to the rigours of the market: competition from new firms is ruled out and inefficiency does not carry the usual penalty of elimination in a struggle for survival.

None of this, however, is inevitable. Several instances of efficient public-sector enterprises are available – the Volkswagen success remaining a constant and rude reminder to *a priori* critics. But note *does* need to be taken of the dangers to which efficiency in these enterprises is subject. Since profitability and the capacity to survive cease to be the regulators of efficiency in the majority of these enterprises, ways of simulating them have been sought by planners everywhere. There are many difficulties here, however. They are most amusingly illustrated by the countless stories, undoubtedly genuine, of Soviet experience. In the publishing sector, for example, a policy of judging (and promoting) efficiency in terms of the number of books published led to a splitting up of books into a large number of volumes. When this was detected, the criterion was shifted to the number of pages printed. This in turn led to wider margins, larger type and greater spaces between lines. The result of these policies, in fact, was that inefficiency and waste were increased rather than reduced!

We have so far argued that profitability is not an imperative for public-sector enterprises. In fact, public-sector investments are likely to be in areas where profitability is in terms of *social* gain rather than financial returns. But this is *different* from arguing that these enterprises *should* make *no* profits at all. Such an argument, though widely held, is unfounded. It has often resulted in the underpricing of the outputs of public-sector enterprises. Aside from the waste of scarce resources implicit in such underpricing, it has also meant that, when public-sector enterprises have produced intermediate items for sale to private industries, the profits foregone by the public sector have accrued to the private sector.

Controls and detailed planning

But the problem of inefficiency remains. And, in many developing countries, it is not a malady of the public sector alone but, indeed, quite universal. It is very important to understand why this is so. It is because these countries use such detailed and comprehensive regulations and controls.

Countries such as India and Ghana have placed fairly comprehensive controls on the entry of firms into industrial activity – except, of course, in cases where small-scale units can multiply and where effective governmental regulation is therefore impossible. Targets are fixed for almost the entire range of industrial activity, and administrative machinery is set up to limit the creation of capacity to the target figures.

This method of industrial licensing often coexists with a situation where industrial targets are so low in relation to the technological processes available that very few plants can be set up in an industry. The targets are low largely because industrialisation is only just beginning to take root, and also because the income levels are not yet high enough to support larger demands. Sometimes targets are set low on social grounds: for example, the productive capacity in

Construction work in progress on the Volta River hydro-electric project in Ghana, one of the most massive enterprises of its kind ever undertaken in Africa or Asia. The picture shows the gigantic conduits through which water flows from the dam to the turbine house.

luxury industries may be limited in the interest of creating an atmosphere of austerity. The phenomenon of industries with very few firms is thus common in developing economies.

In any event, the fortuitous combination of restricted entry and a small number of firms leads to a situation where meaningful competition is impossible and no penalty is imposed (by the market) on inefficiency – a situation analogous to that afflicting public enterprises. This situation, where no inefficient firm has to give way to efficient entrants, is made worse by the way in which other controls are exercised.

It is customary to allocate quotas of foreign exchange to different firms within an industry on a *pro rata* basis. Firms get larger quotas because they have bigger capacities or on the basis of previous allocations. This system again prevents the more efficient firms from bidding successfully for the available exchange. Methods of allocating scarce materials are similar: cement, steel, railway wagons, and so on, are all handed out regardless of efficiency.

The whole system of controls and the *detailed* industrial planning (which they are meant to support) is justified by reference to 'social goals', 'helping the small man to get scarce resources which would otherwise be cornered by big capitalists' and other such criteria. In point of fact, it creates inefficiency, privilege and corruption. There is need to face up to these consequences and to ask whether such detailed targeting and controls are really necessary.

It is difficult to believe that they are. Governments must no doubt ensure that certain basic, key decisions are made. For example, the establishment of a heavy-industry complex must be ensured if it is considered necessary to an eventual increase in the rate of investment. To do this, the public sector may enter these fields and/or private-sector decisions must be influenced and controlled with this purpose in view. This last may mean that resources allowed for setting up light consumer-goods industries must be limited. But to attempt to go *beyond* such key decisions and policies is hardly desirable. To lay down precise targets for *everything* in the industrial sphere, is neither necessary nor capable of

A small-scale industry in Ludhiana in the state of Punjab in India.
Karam Singh is using a lathe to make pistons. His 'Mechanical Works'
have manufactured the lathe as well. The unit occupies only 300 square
feet of floor space and has unplastered walls and a low ceiling.
Note the Sikh saint and a typical Indian calendar on the wall.
Ludhiana is famous in India for its great success with such small enterprises.

yielding any greater rationality than other, decentralised methods of
decision-making. Controls aimed at buttressing these detailed
targets are equally unnecessary and their effects on efficiency and
public morality tend to be an unmitigated disaster.

This is a view which many economists (even when they are
socialists and planners) have begun to hold. They would have
plans worked out much as in chapters 11–16. But they would use
these exercises to take decisions on public-sector investments and
on the broad, economic structure to be imposed on the private
sector. They would *not* bother particularly to waste their own and
other people's time discussing trivialities – such as, for example,
whether toys should be produced and, if so, what the industry's
capacity should be. They would also enable the price mechanism
to play a far greater role. Foreign exchange, cement, steel and
whatever else is scarce would be assured to a *few* 'priority' projects
and be totally refused to certain prohibited categories. But the rest
of these supplies – the bulk – would be allocated through the market. This would certainly introduce some efficiency through competition. It could also earn some revenue for the government (as
when several firms competing for the scarce exchange earmarked
for an industry bid against each other and thereby pass on at least
some of their high profits to the government via higher prices paid
for foreign exchange). The appeal of this non-bureaucratic but
realistic and purposive approach is so great to those who have been
close to the corruption, privilege and inefficiency which have
festered around detailed industrial planning *and* controls in a good
many countries, that it has won many converts..

Unfortunately bureaucrats have a tendency to opt for detailed
targets and comprehensive controls. Many of them are misled by
defunct economic doctrines. A few sense, perhaps, that controls
confer power. Cynics note that their official perquisites are usually
related to ways and means of avoiding these controls (as when,
in India, cars which are otherwise scarce are available to government servants as a priority). Once controls have created privileged
classes – such as the quota-holders of scarce foreign exchange,

whose profits have at times been as high as 300% of the import value in India – they are also politically difficult to eliminate. In this field, it is better to be forewarned. Too much is known now of the gulf between practice and intentions for yet more developing countries to attempt afresh the proliferation of detailed plan-targets and their attendant controls.

Creation of an industrial labour force

One serious difficulty which many developing countries are likely to run into, and which can act as a brake on their industrial efficiency, concerns the availability of a steady labour force. This is *not* the problem of creating skills. Rather it is a question of creating a mass of unskilled operatives who are used to factory hours and the discipline which is so necessary to high productivity and quality of output.

With their rustic backgrounds, the workers take time to adapt themselves to these new conditions of work. The problem of absenteeism, for example, is to be traced to the rural origins of the labour force. But there are problems which are traceable more directly to the process of industrialisation itself. The harshness and cruel rigours of urban life in shanty towns often lead to excessive strain and anguish. These, in turn, have been observed to lead to drunkenness: as in the course of English industrialisation. The early, Czarist period of industrial growth in Russia was also marked, and impeded, by the workers' habitual drunkenness. However, as readers of Dostoyevsky and other Russian writers of the period will readily appreciate, drunkenness was in any case a widespread Russian phenomenon. Indeed, so much so that Russians today amusingly recollect how, if you were looking for a good son-in-law, you never enquired whether he drank; you merely asked how he behaved when he was drunk!

Much of the difficulty, however, in the developing areas is likely to arise from the link which industrial workers frequently continue to maintain with their villages. Many workers leave their families behind for long periods. Many return home for the harvest season. Sometimes workers return permanently to the villages. The recruitment of a strictly urbanised, industrial labour force, which is continuously available for long periods, thus becomes very difficult. The gains which accrue from having a stable labour force over a continued period are hence not so readily available to industrial entrepreneurs in the newly developing countries.

The creation of a highly *skilled* labour force, however, raises somewhat different questions. These are primarily ones of how to gear educational institutions to the growing demand for skilled personnel as industrialisation gathers momentum, and of how to initiate apprenticeship schemes in factories and plants. These questions bring us directly to the whole range of issues concerning the role of education in development.

19 Education and manpower planning

Economists have only recently become aware of the economic effects of social expenditure. Education used to be regarded primarily as an end in itself – with little, if any, effect on productivity. This meant that in the developing countries, educational expenditure was treated as a 'welfare' expenditure for which funds were only grudgingly spared.

However, the shortage of skills and trained manpower and the role played by literacy (and hence by primary education) in promoting population control and agricultural development in these countries have now highlighted the productive (though largely unmeasurable) effects of educational expenditure.

It has even currently become fashionable to compute measures of the 'rate of return' on 'investment' in education. These measures, however, are based on inadequate theories which overlook many important effects of education. Nor do they distinguish between different *types* of education. This latter deficiency is quite serious and, if carried over to the field of educational planning, will produce disastrous results. Expansion in primary education will have quite different effects from an increase in higher education. A system which concentrates on theology and Latin may produce pupils unfit to operate lathes. Resources used for adult education do not carry the same implications as they do when diverted to primary education. Before educational resources are deployed there must be careful consideration of the various alternatives – which depend on the social and economic objectives.

The role of primary education

Most developing countries currently have programmes for universal primary education. This is largely inspired by social considerations, of course. But primary education can prove an excellent vehicle for economic change – particularly if the courses are imaginatively designed. It will be recalled that the Japanese success in rapidly adopting technical improvements in agriculture was facilitated by the slant given to education in the schools.

One of the important issues here relates to the use of resources for primary education. The rate at which primary schools can be multiplied will necessarily be conditioned by the funds available. But in most developing countries, the limitation will be provided by the shortage of teachers. This creates the interesting choice between using teachers to produce more teachers *later* (through teachers' training colleges) and using them *immediately* to expand primary education. This choice between more primary education today and more tomorrow will, in addition, have to be dovetailed into the rate at which *higher* educational facilities are being expanded and will draw on pupils emerging from the primary institutions.

A primary school class in Africa. Education does not depend on expensive buildings.

181

But the use of resources other than teachers also raises some questions of importance. Underdeveloped countries, seeking easy prestige or unthinkingly imitating the trends in affluent countries, have often shown a weakness for expensive buildings – not merely for primary schools but in higher education and indeed throughout the economy. Salaries and maintenance have been poor while colossal and luxurious structures have got lavish allocations of scarce finance. This lopsidedness is disastrous in the poor countries and is an inexcusable waste of resources. One must remember that education can be put across effectively without fine structures – as has been tried in some parts of India. Alternatively, if better buildings *are* desired for political or social reasons, one should think of the cheap, pre-fabricated (but attractively designed) schools which have been judged such an outstanding success in Mexico.

The question of higher education, while raising issues similar to those we have discussed so far, has other important aspects as well, at least two of which need to be discussed, as they are likely to be relevant to most developing countries: the question of general v. technical education and the conflict between quantity and quality.

Technical v. general education

It is only too well known that in the underdeveloped countries which have won their freedom recently from the British and (to a lesser extent) French empires, the attitudes which have developed towards technical education are serious obstacles to the growth of technical skills. The emphasis on arts subjects, the disdain and contempt for technical education, which is often segregated into second-class polytechnics and prevented from taking root in reputable universities, and the almost total exclusion of science and technical graduates from the civil service, were the product of the British cultural and economic environment of the last century. Today they are viewed by most British analysts as a serious cause of the intellectual, scientific and industrial decline of their nation.

These institutions also went very well with the colonial set-up of the underdeveloped countries. But today they stand in the way of progress, diverting much good talent from important technical fields.

Much attention will have to be given in these countries to allocating greater resources *and* conferring greater status on technical and scientific education. There is a pointed moral in the exaggerated comment of Mr Khrushchev:

> We criticised Stalin because he destroyed Lenin's principles of the school system and went back to the classical gymnasium. There they prepared girls for marriage and boys for taking a stroll. They twirled moustaches but still hadn't learnt anything . . . we want people with a deep knowledge of technology.

This technical education will have to be carefully planned. It need hardly be emphasised that such planning calls for a perspective view of the future economy. Some such view is necessary because, without it, no basis exists for the allocation of resources between different types of technical education. The balance of technicians demanded and trained will have to be worked out in some detail, for each category of technician. One of the crucial determinants of the degree of detail in which this planning will have to be done is the specificity of skills. If technicians can move from one industry to another or from one type of job to another, the number of categories planners have to deal with will be correspondingly reduced. Indeed, this will be a great advantage as the view of the future can never be so complete as to make perfect manpower planning possible.

An important aspect of technical education concerns the effective utilisation of talent in the country. Given the educational facilities (e.g. 10,000 admissions per year in the medical colleges) it is necessary to ensure that the most talented and suitable candidates use them. This meritocratic view, of course, assumes that efficiency is important. But it can readily be reconciled with an ethical, egalitarian point of view. Provided merit is distributed randomly among different income-groups *and* is enabled through loans or scholarships, whenever these are necessary, to take advantage of these limited educational facilities, and provided a progressive tax system obtains, the meritocratic system is not altogether prejudicial to average notions of fairness. This argument assumes that a loan or scholarship will be available to the talented poor. Loan schemes, enabling talented but destitute students to go in for higher education, have been traditionally available (through private banks) in the Scandinavian countries. It is surely not beyond the resources of economists in the developing countries to work out schemes which could be adopted by their governments. One possibility, for example, would be to make these loans repayable (and deductible) out of future salaries and the scheme could be made eventually self-financing by working out appropriate rates of loan disbursement and interest and capital repayments.

So far we have been thinking primarily in terms of university and higher education. But industrial expertise also requires that the fullest use be made of opportunities for industrial apprenticeship and learning-on-the-job. In most firms, the intake of apprenticeships for internal use will be less than the capacity to train apprentices. From the social point of view, therefore, it is necessary to persuade or force firms to absorb as many apprentices as possible, provided, of course, they are needed in the economy at large. There is thus a good case for governments, in consultation with industry, to initiate apprenticeship regulations and schemes to make the most of available resources. Industrial training institutes may also have a role to play in this field if adequate apprenticeship facilities are not available. By catering to the more elementary skills in industrial operations, they have been known to supplement the flow of trained personnel to industries in countries such as India and Japan.

Another interesting problem deserves attention with regard to technical education. It concerns the *standards* of education that must be attained and the effect that these have on the important *medical profession*. It is generally conceded in the engineering fields that several possible levels of useful training can be established and that engineers with varying degrees of training are needed on

A craft school for boys in Antakya,
Turkey where instruction is
given in carpentry, ironwork
and the use of machine tools.

different jobs. At each level itself, there is need to maintain efficiency. Thus a bachelor's degree is lower than a master's; but both should be maintained while the absolute standards of each should be preserved. In the medical field, however, such a notion has generally been strongly opposed and in most countries extremely high standards are laid down. Economists have now come to recognise that the medical profession is perhaps one of the most monopolistic 'industries' in non-socialist countries. Under the persuasive guise of 'wanting to save lives', it has imposed highly restricted entry, with resulting high returns. What the public does not realise is that having only highly qualified doctors, with attendant high fees, amounts to depriving poorer patients of the opportunity of having lower-standard but cheaper advice. If a poor man can't consult a doctor, he will have to trust to his grandmother's remedies; and the only choice left him will be between an expensive doctor he cannot afford and no doctor at all. In the Soviet Union, there is a middle category of doctors, who are half-way between nurses and 'first-medical-degree' doctors in the Western countries. When it is recalled that much medicine today is patented and that a proper network of consultation up to higher levels could be established for more complicated cases, there is no reason why governments of the developing countries should surrender to pressures from the medical lobby and not emulate the Soviet example.

Quantity v. quality

Although it is possible to plan so as to aim at matching the supply and demand of skilled personnel as the economy progresses, the practical problems can be acute and may prevent rational planning. Thus, for example, there is a tremendous demand in the developing countries for more higher-education institutions. Instead of trying to produce graduates and technicians who are both well-trained and just sufficiently numerous to be absorbed in the growing economy, the politicians in these countries typically opt simply for more admissions and more institutions.

As a result the ratio of teachers to students falls. The quality of teachers drops. And the stream of students, no matter how low their average intelligence and aptitude for higher education, has to be got through the examinations – a high failure rate would be politically suicidal. These factors, resulting from a thin spread of limited educational resources, combine to produce impossibly large numbers of 'qualified' young men and women who add up to a statistically impressive, but misleading figure of planned achievement in education. They expect jobs commensurate with their attainment but they cannot all be absorbed. The resulting mass of frustrated graduates obviously spells danger to political stability.

The only rational course of action is to resist these pressures for higher education. The politicians must be firm. Or, alternatively, the educational institutions, when they have autonomy, must insist on a saner course of action. But if the expansion cannot be resisted, at least the *economic* waste, implicit in the general lowering of standards, must be avoided. It is worth considering how this can be done – as it is all that is likely to be possible in some of the underdeveloped countries.

In the majority of English-tradition countries, universities are also examining bodies. The growth of colleges, affiliated to these universities, inevitably leads to lower standards all round because of bad entrants. The best solution under these circumstances is *not* to use the federal structure at all. As in Japan and the United States, each new college should be permitted to run its own instruction and examinations. *Its* standards, if bad, will not then affect those of the other, better institutions. It is only when everyone has to swim together that the good institutions suffer from the bad. A scheme of decentralisation would at least preserve the better ones.

But it must be emphasised again that this decentralisation cannot prevent the explosive effects that a mass of inferior graduates, faced with the prospects of unemployment or of employment which they consider unsuitable to their educated status, holds out for these countries. This political danger, no less than the economic waste of resources that such an educational system entails, needs to be fully appreciated. And safeguards must be developed appropriate to each country.

Fundamental v. applied research

Underdeveloped countries also need to guard against an excessive use of resources in 'basic research'. Once again, the countries which have inherited British intellectual traditions are found to be particularly vulnerable to the temptation to pursue fundamental, abstruse research which is unrelated, at least immediately, to the problems of these countries.

Such an orientation towards research is undoubtedly good in the very long run. The most esoteric research has a habit of impinging on reality in unforeseen ways. Despite this, however, it hardly helps to solve pressing technological problems. A willingness to regard 'applied' research as comparable, in terms of complexity and intellectual challenge, to fundamental research is thus essential. Underdeveloped countries should consciously pursue policies designed to support, rather than negate, such an orientation.

A clearly defined educational policy, integrated *at several levels* with the perspective view of the economy and the social framework, will thus have to be pursued. The numerous *alternatives* which obtain in this area will have to be carefully considered, and decisions will have to be taken which will promote social and economic objectives.

Important choices are also available to planners in other areas of the economy. We now proceed to analyse some of these, starting with those relating to technology.

20 The choice of technology

In technology, the question of choice is extremely significant. Technological choices exist at several levels, although they are most readily associated with the availability of alternative designs for specific *projects*.

In the case of practically any project, it is possible to substitute one method of production for another. In electricity generation, for example, we can choose among thermal plants, hydral stations and atomic energy units. The possibility of substitution exists in such instances at the level of different processes involving different *types* of capital equipment and plant.

However, even when a specific process has been chosen for a project, it is possible to find still further possibilities of choice. Among these, at least eight interesting ways in which these choices arise can be spelled out.

1 A plant can be operated at one or more shifts. In some industries, such as steel and chemicals, continuous production is technologically required. But for many others, there is a genuine choice here. Operating the plant at more than one shift implies a more intensive use of the equipment and is, for this reason, more economical whenever capital is more expensive than labour. Except in cases where heavy overtime rates have to be paid to labour during the extra shift(s) or where machinery needs to be rested for long periods after a shift (as is frequently the case with old machines), it should be profitable for a firm to use more shifts as long as it can sell its output. Interestingly enough, this is underlined by English experience in the early nineteenth century. In the agitation against the Factory Acts, the objection of many English manufacturers to the shortening of hours by legislation was not so much that it would increase labour-costs per hour – because many manufacturers expected wages to fall in proportion – but that it would limit the hours they could run their machinery and so would increase capital-costs per unit of output. Hansard records Sir James Graham's objection that the proposed legislation would 'abridge the hours your machinery is to run by no less than one-sixth part'.

But while it should normally pay firms to operate multiple shifts, things do not always work out that way. It is often the case, for instance, that firms in an industry are traditionally used to working only one shift and have never thought of doing otherwise. Alternatively, many firms find it too bothersome to organise extra shifts and would rather forgo the extra profits that multiple shifts would bring. Or some firms, from moral and social considerations, do not like to have workers at jobs during the night. In all these cases, the *social* desirability of having multiple shifts (to economise on the use of capital in labour-abundant areas) will not be served by private decisions. Economists have thus recommended the use of fiscal policy to *induce* the wider adoption of multiple shifts in these cases. Inducements could take the form, for example, of a tax benefit related to the working of more shifts. Alternatively, penalties could be directly imposed on firms working fewer shifts. In the developing countries where industrial licencing controls are used, the authorities could make the working of more shifts a condition for these licences.

2 Another choice that exists concerns the *speed* at which machinery is worked. In some processes, it is possible to increase speed, while reducing the number of men who will attend the machine. An English observer of the American textile industry in 1854 noted:

'The general speed of power-looms, and indeed of machinery generally, is lower than in England. By this means labour is economised, and one labourer can attend to more machines. . . . Since running machinery more slowly is a method of saving labour at the expense of an increase in capital per unit of output, it is what we should expect in a country of dear labour.

3 The possibility of choice arises also through 'breakdowns' of machinery. Equipment does not suddenly disintegrate *at the end* of a specified period. Machines break down periodically, despite proper maintenance. Since these breakdowns cannot be foreseen completely, and since they may 'bunch together', the firm has the option of having *either* a large crew of repair personnel which can quickly take care of bunched breakdowns *or* a smaller crew which takes longer to handle the job at peak hours. The former alternative

involves leaving some *crew* idle at non-peak times; the latter implies leaving some *machinery* idle at peak times. The choice will thus turn on the relative costs of these two possible decisions.

4 Such a choice arises again in the case of holidays and rest periods. We have previously noted (see chapter 7) how rest periods for workers can leave machinery idle and that firms might well find it more economical to have a few extra labourers to keep the machinery running during these periods. This alternative would, of course, leave these workers idle during the rest of the working day. The choice is even more important when the annual holidays of workers are considered. Most firms prefer to stagger holidays so as to avoid unnecessary shutting-down of the plant. Some firms, however, are known to close for a short period annually: they are usually in industries where machinery has to be overhauled during this period *in any case*, or where the proportion of capital to labour is low so that it is more economical to leave capital idle than labour.

5 Further, even when the manufacturing equipment has been chosen, it is frequently possible to combine factors of production in different proportions for incidental operations. In packaging, delivery and so on, it is possible to use more labour-intensive methods. These are, in fact, among the principal ways in which some chemical firms (such as ICI and I.G.Farben) have been known to adapt their techniques when operating subsidiaries in labour-abundant countries. An alternative example is provided by the combination of high dams with labour-intensive methods of getting water from feeder canals to individual farms.

6 Choices are also available with respect to the *length of life* of the plant. A thermal station can be built to last over varying periods. The corresponding costs will also differ. And, in some instances, the operating expenses per unit of output also will vary with the durability of equipment.

7 The question of longevity, however, can be distinguished from that of *maintenance*. A machine may be built to last ten years, provided it is maintained at a specific standard. However, by varying the degree of maintenance, we can alter the effective life of the

machine. A bus, if properly maintained, may last fifteen years. If not, it may last only half the time. Thus the *level* of maintenance itself is subject to selection with a view to increasing economic efficiency.

8 Finally, the *size* of the plant and the method of its expansion also offer possibilities of efficient choice. In an earlier chapter (chapter 16) we have referred to conditions under which it may be more economical to build plants which have uneconomic costs because of their small scale of production. We noted how the geographical distribution of demand may be such that several scattered, small plants may save more on *transportation* costs than they lose on *production* costs. Similarly, the pattern of increase in demand may, *over time*, be such as to make it economical to erect large plants which have *excess capacity* over shorter periods, in preference to small plants which do not create excess capacity and are expanded to match increasing demand as and when it materialises.

Technological choice within an activity is thus available in numerous ways. However, it is even wider than the preceding analysis suggests. The alternatives we have discussed so far were concerned exclusively with different ways in which *identical products* may be produced. These related to different processes and to different ways in which the same process may still leave open further possibilities of selection.

But technological alternatives are sometimes associated with variations in the product itself. There are two principal ways in which this may be so.

First, one process may result in a *better-quality* product. For example, automatic looms produce more attractive textiles. This can be quite an important factor in the choice of technique. In India, for instance, by subsidising labour-intensive, cottage-industry techniques in spinning and weaving and restricting the instalment of automatic looms the capacity of the industry to compete with Japanese exports in foreign markets has been significantly impaired. If enough weight is attached to export earnings, the

Indian planners' choice of this technique could well turn out to be misguided and inefficient.

Secondly, processes may differ in the number of *by-products* that they can harness. An appropriate example is provided by the contrast between beehive coking-ovens and modern processes. The former process, still in vogue in many developing countries such as China and India, wastes the gases which yield many valuable chemical products – whose value may be as high as 50% of the coking coal produced. These by-products are utilised by the modern processes which, however, require substantially more capital.

The question of the choice of technique in most economic activities is thus fairly complex. Economists, recognising this, have given much attention to methods of 'project analysis' so as to be able to choose efficiently from the numerous alternatives available. These methods are basically similar to those we have already touched upon in chapter 11. They are most profitably illustrated by analysing two important factors relevant to planning in the under-developed areas: 1 the role of small industry; and 2 the possibility of using second-hand machines.

Small-scale units have usually been recommended, mainly on the ground that they create more employment. This claim, however, needs to be carefully examined. In the Indian context, for example, it was found that many of the cottage-industry, labour-intensive techniques were so primitive and inefficient in relation to modern processes that they used more of *both* capital *and* labour to produce the same output. With given capital, therefore, these techniques produced lower output and thereby reduced economic efficiency significantly. Also, by increasing the share of wages in this reduced quantum of output, these techniques cut into savings and accumulation out of *profits*, thereby reducing not merely current output but also the capacity to grow faster and hence create greater employment opportunities in the long run.

What underdeveloped countries need are techniques which are labour-intensive in the sense that they substitute labour for capital *and* which are also efficient in terms of productivity. Experiments

have been made in Japan and India, for example, where simple adjustments such as the fitting of electric motors to spinning wheels have sometimes been very successful. It is really up to the labour-abundant, developing countries to direct their scientific research to turning out superior, labour-intensive techniques. Many of the scientific innovations in the developed countries so far have been capital-using and aimed at *reducing* labour requirements.

The question of quality needs to be stressed again in this context. Techniques used in small industries often produce less attractive results than modern technology used in larger units. This can affect export markets, as with Indian textiles. Or it can lead to considerable *waste*. The Chinese campaign to produce *quality* pig iron in incredibly small and scattered smelting furnaces reportedly led to disastrous results. It is impossible to control quality in these small, unmechanised processes. This expensive experiment provides an

Blast-furnaces in backyards. This Chinese campaign to increase iron output, which resulted both in overproduction and in waste through bad quality, is a good example of how *not* to pursue the search for labour-intensive techniques in labour-abundant areas.

excellent illustration of how the small-industry approach should *not* be used.

What has attracted some planners to small industries is the hope that they may stem the flow of surplus labour from rural to urban areas. In giant cities such as Calcutta, the seething mass of unemployed immigrants has created appalling conditions which will bring disaster unless they are speedily eliminated. Some social analysts have even suggested the establishment of a network of small towns, with small-scale industries, to absorb the migrant, rural labour. The economic advantage of *rural* industries, however, is that (provided they are based on easily transportable raw materials *or* on local materials and markets) they can be set up without the need for extensive new building. It is well known that the factory towns of the early British industrial revolution absorbed considerable quantities of capital. The rural industries are also likely to act as catalysts in the agricultural revolution. In the ultimate choice between small and large industries, these larger questions have to be borne in mind.

The question of using second-hand equipment is relatively easier to analyse. Owing to rapid obsolescence, many advanced countries scrap machinery when its technical life is yet unspent. Underdeveloped countries could import such equipment and find it more economical than buying new machines. When machines have been scrapped by industries in countries where wages are relatively high, their use in the underdeveloped countries where labour is relatively cheaper, should also be economical. The possibility of such advantageous imports extends also to durable consumer goods where new models send the prices of the older models tumbling down in affluent countries such as the United States.

There are only two difficulties which seem to reduce the attractiveness of such imports. First, there may be difficulties in getting spare parts for old machinery and durables. Second, the equipment is likely to have been roughly used, in view of its rapid obsolescence, and may demand considerable maintenance which may be a scarce and expensive resource in underdeveloped countries. These factors may well outweigh the advantages of employing used machines and durables, but not necessarily. To those who have seen the rapid growth of small, machine and metal-working units in the underdeveloped countries, and the facility with which old buses and equipment are kept going in these areas, there seems great room for optimism.

In fact, it would be highly profitable for the developing countries to look systematically into possibilities of importing used equipment and to work out the relevant economics in each specific context. It may even be useful, in this connection, to explore the Army Surplus Disposal programmes, which are an immensely rich source of bargains in the United States, for example. An imaginative and careful approach to this unexplored question could pay very rich dividends.

21 Reducing the birth rate

For a large number of underdeveloped countries, there is an important choice in the use of resources for reducing the growth of population. Indeed, it is vitally necessary for countries with severe underemployment and rapidly growing populations to consider the question of population control with the utmost seriousness. Unfortunately, even countries in serious population difficulties (as, for example, India) have contented themselves with cursory analysis and inadequate action in this important field.

One of the most meaningful ways in which the problem of choice can be posed in this area is to investigate the *alternative effects* of using resources for population control and for income expansion. Among these alternatives, the most compelling seem to be the resulting per capita income over a period and the rate at which it can be expected to rise subsequently. Obviously, other aspects of these alternatives may be considered equally or more important: as is implicitly the case when a population policy is ruled out on social criteria.

Some people argue that it is nonsensical to consider a population policy for the underdeveloped countries. History, they say, has frequently demonstrated the close link that exists between high incomes and low birth rates – a relationship that seems to be reversed as incomes reach the levels of truly affluent societies such as the United States today. If birth rates will not fall unless incomes have *already* risen significantly, it is a waste of time to suggest population control to the governments of the low-income, developing countries.

This view is buttressed by the argument that, in many underdeveloped countries, there are a number of socio-economic factors which make a high birth rate inevitable. The desire to have a surviving son, and religious taboos against interference with procreative functions are significant in many countries. Peasant families, even if progressive, are likely to find more children useful: they provide security in old age and they can assist on the farm (while their 'cost' to the family is marginal and hence negligible). In any case, it is impossible to expect progressive attitudes in the developing countries when illiteracy rates are so high. For much the same reason, even population control campaigns would meet with little response, except over an impossibly long period (during which literacy is increased and sustained propaganda efforts are made).

These views certainly seem persuasive. But they are debatable. To begin with, historical experience is hardly an adequate guide in a field where *governmental action* has been notoriously absent, or, when undertaken, negligible and disorganised (despite professions to the contrary). Moreover, while social factors (such as illiteracy and religious attitudes) may seriously inhibit the success of a campaign which is aimed *exclusively* at disseminating information and exhorting people to have smaller families, this cannot rule out the possibility of successfully providing *economic* incentives to promote a fall in the birth rate.

Far too many campaigns for population control have been confined to education and appeal – a process which is necessarily slow and ineffective over periods of less than fifteen years. Sometimes they have been abandoned too soon (as in China), and sometimes they have been too diffuse (as in India). Often the social factors to which they must be adapted for maximum success have been little understood.

The chances of a population policy succeeding cannot, therefore, be so readily ruled out. It remains sensible to propose such a policy as an alternative way of using (some) resources in developing economies. How then can a government carry out a population control programme quickly and economically?

Of course the precise contents of a population policy will vary with local conditions. No programme is likely to be suitable both to Indonesia and to Burma, for example. What *can* be done, however, is to discuss certain general, but important, issues suggested by experience and reflection.

There are two different aspects of an effective population control programme: 1 methods of birth control; and 2 the ways in which people can be persuaded to adopt them. Among the former, the serious alternatives concern different methods of contraception, abortion and sterilisation. Among the latter, we have to consider primarily the role of literacy, propaganda, medical centres and economic incentives (e.g. bonus schemes for smaller families).

The choice between different methods of birth control turns on two different issues: 1 their social acceptability; and 2 their efficacy. Unfortunately, with the current state of medical knowledge, the methods of fertility control which are likely to be most effective in the developing countries are also those which are open to serious moral objection.

The contraceptive method is among the most difficult to put across to illiterate and impoverished families. Time and again, experiments with foam tablets, diaphragms, prophylactics, and the rhythm method have shown disappointing results. The chief difficulties stem from the need for recurrent and regular use, inadequate understanding of the methods and subconscious inhibitions to some of them. These are the factors which have prompted the search for *oral* and other contraceptives.

In addition to these, however, the Japanese method of legalising abortions and the practice of sterilisation (begun recently in India), providing possibilities of effective birth control, need to be carefully considered. The objections to both practices are moral. Abortions are unacceptable to orthodox opinion in many Western countries of Christian persuasion and are, of course, ruled out for Catholics. The objection to sterilisation, on the other hand, stems from liberalism rather than religious attitudes. Although sterilisation operations are reversible in some cases, from the individual's point of view it is relevant to consider that they *could* be irreversible. This irreversibility is considered by liberal opinion to be seriously prejudicial to the case for making sterilisation facilities available.

However, neither of these moral objections is seriously entertained in a large number of the developing countries. They are not therefore likely to stand in the way of the adoption of abortion and sterilisation in these countries. And, in fact, these expedients should be given the utmost consideration by these countries – since exclusive reliance on the traditional, Western practice of birth control through contraceptive methods is the least suitable and the most difficult way of controlling the birth rate in the developing countries today.

Experience also indicates the importance of literacy and education in getting wider and readier acceptance of birth control. This is naturally not sufficient in itself; but it helps. The expenditure on raising the level of literacy in the developing countries is thus to be considered not merely as an end in itself but also, among other things, as a powerful lever in increasing the effectiveness of population control campaigns. The interesting questions to consider concerning the methods of securing acceptance of birth control relate to issues other than literacy and education.

To begin with, it is necessary to ensure that the notion of family planning is put across intelligibly *and* continuously over a longish period. Thus it is *not* enough for a government official merely to visit an area, hold a few meetings, talk about contraception and sterilisation facilities at a clinic and leave matters there (as has happened only too frequently in India). The question of family planning is so delicate that a continuous and intensive coverage, including several follow-up visits, are absolutely indispensable to a serious campaign. It is also necessary to decide carefully whether public meetings or door-to-door calls are preferable. It has been claimed, on the basis of experience in some Indian villages, that individuals are shy on their own and find a public meeting useful as a way of overcoming their inhibitions. This seems doubtful, however; and education of individual families is likely to be more advantageous and economical in results (although apparently more expensive).

But even this is unlikely to be adequate for illiterate populations. It hardly needs to be emphasised that the question is fraught with psychological difficulties. Sterilisation, for example, may be equated subconsciously with impotence. There are also likely to be other fears which cannot be removed *merely* by government officials and field-workers. For example, the effect of abortions (and even of contraception) on health may be a cause for worry. On these and other issues, it is clear that what is important is the kind of relationship that exists between doctor and patient. Unless there is *confidence* in those administering it, the success of a family planning scheme will be severely limited.

The case for operating clinics devoted *exclusively* to family planning is therefore weak. It is much more sensible to make them an *integral* part of medical centres so that the medical staff can take advantage of their position to suggest and encourage family planning. This would be desirable on two other grounds as well. 1 The occupation of midwifery has a stake in higher birth rates and in backward areas midwives may be directly interested in frustrating family planning campaigns. They have been known to play on the fears and complexes of illiterate parents. Only doctors and nurses who have won the confidence of their patients will be able to meet this powerful source of counter-propaganda. 2 Moreover, in many societies, there are inhibitions against being *known* to practice family planning. It is, therefore, rather naïve to expect that parents will readily go to clinics exclusively geared to family planning. It would be much more sensible to make family planning advice and methods available *in the course of* treatment of (apparent or real) ill-health.

It would be excellent, moreover, to integrate these medical centres with *bonus schemes* for smaller families. Western countries have experimented with family allowances to provide incentives for *larger* families. This notion can be inverted so that schemes are devised to induce smaller families. Such incentive schemes raise two different issues: one concerning the form in which benefits are given and the other concerning their size.

Benefits can be paid either in cash or in specific forms such as an assigned number of free medical visits to the centre. The latter is psychologically a more powerful inducement: parents are likely to restrain the size of their families if the health and well-being of their existing children are explicitly at stake.

The size of the benefits can be adjusted, with experience, to the level at which results are likely to follow. The pattern of such benefits will also have to take into account the *expected fertility* of families in different age-groups and their departure from it (making allowance for factors such as sterility). Such schemes have in fact been worked out by several analysts, although none has been put to the test of actual experimentation. Only recently, the Indian government has begun to provide straightforward, unvarying and small cash benefits to those opting for sterilisation. There thus remains great scope for a more systematic and ambitious use of incentive schemes.

Needless to say, these tasks of educating parents, securing their willingness to control family size, and ensuring that they really do control it are extremely complex and require careful thought. The complexities of population control are admirably underlined by the story about the Indian poster which contrasted a family of two in an enviable cottage with a family of six in a squalid hut. A peasant, looking at this deliberate accentuation of the misery of larger families, shook his head and sighed: 'What a pity! Such a nice house and only two children!'

22 The political economy of development

We have already observed the close interaction that exists between the economic system and the political framework and ethos within which it operates and to which it contributes. But the point is so important that it is worth analysing in greater detail.

One of the most difficult questions raised by development concerns its effect on the distribution of wealth. Rapid growth, in a mixed economy, with private ownership of property and the means of production, produces conditions under which concentration of wealth and economic power are likely to thrive. There are several reasons for this phenomenon. The primary factor, however, is the scarcity of private entrepreneurs with both organising ability *and* financial resources. Often, even when the number of entrepreneurs is more numerous, the licensing authorities find the bigger and established firms more efficient and therefore regard them as better candidates. Typically, therefore, a few business 'houses' develop extensive industrial, financial and trading interests. In India, for example, the topmost business complexes have amassed capital investments which are not merely immense in relation to national wealth but also extensive in their range. This situation leads, in the first place, to monopolistic practices which may be economically inefficient – a result which must be weighed against the advantages of more efficient organisation and management which these business houses may offer. More important, these large complexes develop considerable political influence. After a certain stage it becomes impossible to reverse the political situation by evolutionary, reformist methods: the government becomes dependent for party finance on economic giants and impervious to any *genuine* control of the concentration of wealth and economic power.

The close link which develops between vested interests and governments is worrying not merely in itself but because it threatens eventually to stand in the way of economic progress. Growing concentration of wealth and influence, for example, shields the wealthier classes from heavy taxation. This in turn prevents governments from taxing other, not-so-affluent groups. The whole tax effort thus gets compromised. And so on.

In fact, the existence of vested interests and pressure groups holds up economic progress over a vast range of issues. Land reform is a typical example. Frequently, stiff legislation is put on the statute books to silence radical criticism. In practice, the legislation is implemented with cynicism and widely avoided.

This raises a more general point. Practically no measure aimed at economic progress will be universally beneficial. Some individuals and classes will gain and others will lose. It is rarely practicable to compensate the losers. Thus, no policy of economic development can be carried out unless the government has the capacity to adhere to it, no matter how organised and systematic the opposition to it by the losers – who may well be powerful pressure groups. Quite often, however, democratic governments lose equanimity and determination in the face of opposition. In the Indian case, for example, measures aimed at reducing wasteful expenditure on gold and increasing savings through a compulsory deposit scheme were substantially withdrawn in the light of public agitation, despite a state of emergency in the country.

This is the dilemma of most democratic governments. While the majority of the electorate certainly want rapid economic progress, few of them are willing to concede that the government's measures to achieve it are either necessary or desirable. It is common practice, for example, for people to criticise taxation while becoming indignant about the poverty which that taxation is aimed at eliminating. It is not surprising that most democratic governments, even when enlightened and willing to initiate and encourage economic progress, feel it necessary to go about their business with caution and often to retreat from sound policies.

It is here that socialist countries, such as the Soviet Union and mainland China, have an immense advantage: their totalitarian structure shields the government from the rigorous and reactionary judgments of the electorate. The Soviet government's firm control on expansion in consumption over the last few decades could hardly ever be attempted by a democratic government. Another advantage of the socialist countries is their passionate conviction and dedication to the objective of economic growth – which contrasts visibly with the halting and hesitant beliefs and actions of most democracies. The firm and purposive sense of direction which the Chinese maintained through the early 1960's, in the face of floods, drought and other economic disasters, is in pointed contrast to the extensive revisions and changes in policies and methods which are prompted by minor setbacks in most democratic governments and which produce a sense of drift and helplessness.

The political economy of development poses, in this respect, a cruel choice between rapid (self-sustained) expansion and democratic processes. The choice between them, however, is not necessarily unique; and rightly so.

PART FOUR

The international framework

23 International transfer of resources

The process of transforming the underdeveloped countries can be accelerated significantly by adjusting the international framework within which their economies are set. These adjustments relate to questions of trade, as well as to the international transfer of resources from the advanced to the underdeveloped regions. It is necessary, therefore, to consider both these aspects at length.

The flow of resources between countries has three essential facets, of equal significance from the point of view of the developing countries: 1 capital movements; 2 sharing of technical knowledge; and 3 transfer of skilled personnel. Each raises questions of interest and importance; and suggestions for reform of current international institutions can be made in respect of all of them. We begin with the international transfer of capital.

Capital flow to the underdeveloped countries consists of *official* grants and loans and *private* investments. Though they raise some similar problems it is convenient to treat them separately.

Official capital transfers

The most striking feature of official capital flows to the underdeveloped countries is their inadequacy. Not that the overall flow of official and private capital to the developing countries today compares particularly unfavourably with that in the nineteenth century, when considered as a proportion of world trade. It does not. Its insufficiency relates to the needs of the underdeveloped countries *and* to the ability of the advanced countries to pay.

Foreign trade permits the transformation, through exchange, of a country's output into those commodities that it needs. Countries undergoing rapid economic expansion usually find it necessary to import considerable quantities of capital goods and raw materials which their economies demand but are not geared to produce. Unfortunately, estimates of the import requirements of most underdeveloped countries have consistently been greater than any reasonable estimate of the expansion that their export earnings can register! Measures will no doubt have to be taken to adjust the international economy so that it generates a sufficient increase in exports from the developing countries in the long run; and this is a subject we shall explore at length later (in chapter 25). Measures to increase the flow of *private* investment will also be necessary.

In the immediate future, however, grants and loans will have to fill the gap in foreign exchange resources. For those underdeveloped countries which can make the necessary savings effort at home, this is the primary rationale of foreign aid. But to the many countries which find domestic savings difficult to mobilise rapidly, the fact that foreign aid *also* means additional savings is of equal, if not greater, significance. Indeed, economists have also attempted estimates of foreign aid, based on the calculated differences between the savings required for ensuring satisfactory rates of growth in the underdeveloped areas and their likely domestic savings.

It is perhaps significant that *both* the approaches to the calculation of foreign aid required by the underdeveloped countries – that based on their import requirements and alternatively on the short-fall in their domestic savings – throw up magnitudes which make the recent flows of capital appear inadequate. However, these estimates are generally biased on the higher side. After all, most of them come *either* from the underdeveloped countries themselves *or* from international organisations whose experts and staff are emotionally committed to larger aid flows *or* from liberal economists and writers; the conservatives have a long-standing habit of refusing to discuss these questions except at an abstract level and on an *a priori* basis. Yet even after allowance has been made for the upward bias of the estimates, we still cannot fail to be impressed by the gap between the capital flow required and its present level. Take for example one of the recent estimates, coming from an eminent American economist and using the savings-requirements approach. It places the annual capital-flow requirement of the under-developed countries for the decade 1961–71 at a level which exceeds the comparable flow in 1961 by over 50%. (The projected distribution to recipients is also interesting: see figure 28). With reasonable estimates of increases in *private investment*, this leaves us with an estimate of the required increase in *foreign aid* of at least the same proportion.

Again, judged in relation to the advanced countries' *ability to pay*, the recent size of capital movements is equally unimpressive. Many approaches to this question are naturally possible – as to the question of the ability to pay of different income-classes *within* a nation. For example, many liberals (including progressive opinion in the British Labour Party) have supported a foreign aid target of 1% of G.N.P. for every advanced country.

But since it presupposes a *proportional* method of burden-sharing such a proposal is unlikely to be universally acceptable. Several analysts actually prefer a *progressive* method of burden-sharing, with the richer nations bearing a higher proportion of the cost of an international aid programme, and paying a higher percentage of their G.N.P., much as the higher-income classes are taxed at progressively higher rates *within* a country. This approach has been explored in an interesting recent analysis of ten important advanced countries. Several alternative estimates of cost-sharing among them were made, using proportional taxation, as in the 1% of G.N.P. plan, and the progressive tax rates of the United Kingdom, West Germany and the United States, successively on individual and then on national incomes. The results were then compared with these nations' *actual shares* in aid to under-developed countries in 1960 (see figure 29). One of the interesting things that emerged was that, by these criteria, the share of the United States in aid programmes is not excessive, as is generally believed, but actually falls on the low side!

While foreign aid needs to be substantially expanded, and the distribution of its cost has to be carefully looked into, there are many respects in which its effectiveness can be increased from the points of view of both the recipient and the donor countries. There are at least four major areas in which such reform would be useful. These relate to: 1 the tying of aid; 2 the issue of multilateral v. bilateral aid; 3 the difficulty of repayment of aid; and 4 the commitment of aid over longer periods of time.

Figure 28. *One estimate of the requirements of long-term capital inflow per annum into underdeveloped countries, 1961–6 and 1966–71.*
One of several, it is based on the approach which estimates required aid as the difference between savings required to promote development and the savings that can be raised within the underdeveloped countries themselves. Alternative estimates, using other criteria and methods, are possible.

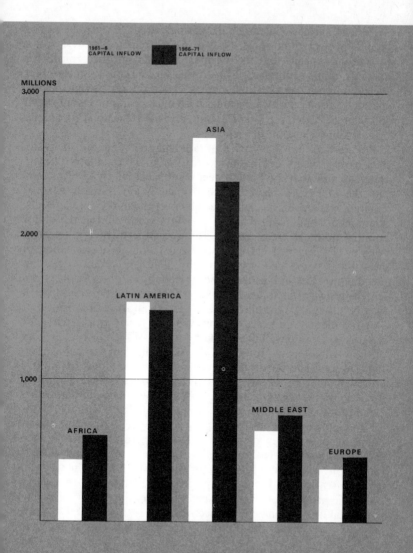

Foreign aid has come to be increasingly 'tied'. Aid can be tied to specific projects; and it can be tied to the donor country. Tying it to a project means that the aid must be spent on the project: for example, on its equipment. Tying it to a specific country means that the aid must be spent on that country's goods alone: the machinery, materials, food on which the aid is used must be imported only from this source. Both these practices have an obvious rationale from the donor country's point of view.

Project-tied aid has political advantages. The aid is easily identifiable when attributed to projects. Thus, many literate Indians know that the Bhillai Steel plant was built by the Russians and the Durgapur plant by the British. If aid is scattered over different small projects, and especially over the import of materials, components and spare parts, it does not readily bring the donor country political credit at the same mass level in the recipient country. Project-tied aid has also been favoured as a method of ensuring that aid gets spent usefully. Thus, in order to prevent the dictatorship in the Dominican Republic, for example, from frittering away aid funds on luxury imports and consumption, it may be thought advisable to link the aid to an irrigation project or a textile factory. In practice, however, this rarely works out – for reasons which are well illustrated by the possibly apocryphal story of the Vienna Opera House and the Marshall Plan for reconstructing Europe. The Austrian government was planning to build a power plant from its own funds and wished to use Marshall Plan funds to rebuild the Opera House. When the American authorities failed to see that the Opera House was essential and withheld funds for this purpose, the Austrian government merely switched their financing plans: they reconstructed the Opera House from their own funds (previously earmarked for the power plant) and successfully secured Marshall Plan aid for the power plant! The moral is clear: attention to individual projects is inadequate; the *entire* economic programme of the recipient country must be studied. The corresponding rationale of project-tied aid is therefore also weak.

Aid is tied to the donor country for different reasons but with similar weaknesses. The primary reason for country-tied aid is perhaps political, stemming from pressure groups interested in export markets. But it is strongly buttressed by economic arguments. Suppose that United States aid to Indonesia were spent on German machinery. This would mean that the Germans would be accumulating dollars which they could present to the American authorities for conversion into marks or gold. This would probably create balance of payments difficulties for America. To prevent such difficulties American aid might be tied to American goods.

But the economic rationale is weaker than it appears, for the same reason as in the case of project-tied aid: switches may occur here as well. If the aid has to be spent on United States goods alone whereas Indonesia would like to spend it in Germany, Indonesia could well divert her *previous* imports from the United States to Germany and *de facto* use the aid for German goods. Thus, for example, Indonesia may be spending $50 million on imports of wheat from the United States. If aid of $50 million is now available but tied to the United States, Indonesia could merely use the $50 million aid to purchase wheat from the United States and spend the $50 million *released* to buy machinery from Germany (rather than from the United States). This example presupposes adequate *previous* imports from the donor country. It also assumes that the United States aid is not tied to specific projects. If the aid had also been tied to a project, and thence to imports of electrical machinery for instance, the dodge by Indonesia would have been *impossible* in the example chosen. The switch in such an instance would be permissible *only* if the previous imports from the United States consisted of electrical machinery (rather than wheat). In so far as switches take place, the primary economic purpose of country-tied aid is frustrated. But to the extent that they do not, the procedure creates difficulties for the recipient country.

Indeed, *both* project-tied and country-tied aid limit the effectiveness of assistance to the recipient countries. Take project-tied aid. Indian experience during 1956–65 highlights the impossible situation that the system can generate. The Indian planners repeatedly

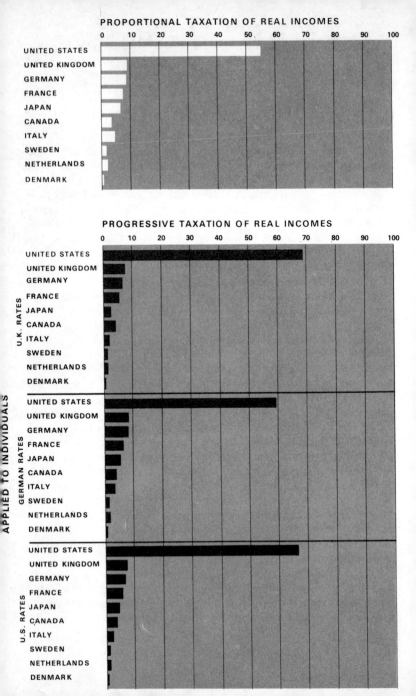

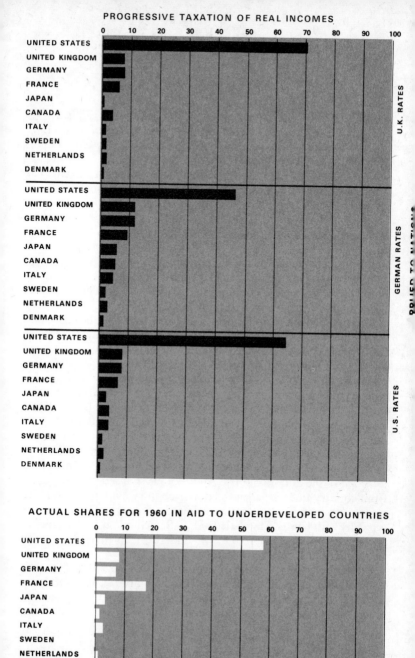

PROGRESSIVE TAXATION OF REAL INCOMES

U.K. RATES

UNITED STATES
UNITED KINGDOM
GERMANY
FRANCE
JAPAN
CANADA
ITALY
SWEDEN
NETHERLANDS
DENMARK

GERMAN RATES

UNITED STATES
UNITED KINGDOM
GERMANY
FRANCE
JAPAN
CANADA
ITALY
SWEDEN
NETHERLANDS
DENMARK

U.S. RATES

UNITED STATES
UNITED KINGDOM
GERMANY
FRANCE
JAPAN
CANADA
ITALY
SWEDEN
NETHERLANDS
DENMARK

ACTUAL SHARES FOR 1960 IN AID TO UNDERDEVELOPED COUNTRIES

UNITED STATES
UNITED KINGDOM
GERMANY
FRANCE
JAPAN
CANADA
ITALY
SWEDEN
NETHERLANDS
DENMARK

found that while they had enough foreign exchange to set up *additional capacity*, they had none to utilise even their existing industrial capacity fully! The net result in such cases is to reduce drastically the effectiveness of foreign aid.

There are two ways of getting round this inefficient system. The simplest thing to do, naturally, is to have large components of aid given for 'general purpose' imports – a practice which may gain acceptance now that the United States has begun to adopt it. The alternative, which may be politically easier, is to 'weaken' the notion of a project so that it includes a number of incidental and supplementary activities: thus an alumina plant 'project' will include bauxite mining, power plant, transport facilities and so on. Both these ways of softening the impact of the project-tying system need to be widely accepted.

Country-tied aid also frequently imposes an economic cost upon the recipient countries when switching is not possible. There are two principal ways in which this happens. First, purchases from the donor country may be more expensive. This is a frequent complaint against United States-tied aid: prices in that country, for most types of machinery, seem to compare unfavourably with European and Japanese prices. The high cost can arise from relative inefficiency or inflation. It is also explained sometimes by the monopolistic selling which may occur once it is known that the order for a project must be placed in the country. Instances have been known of collusive tendering to recipients of aid tied to projects *and* to the donor country. An economic burden may also arise from country-tied aid when the donor country employs productive techniques inapproriate to the recipient's economy. This happens typically with United States-tied aid. U.S. technology is often highly automated and less suitable to the underdeveloped countries than European and Japanese techniques.

From the point of view of economic efficiency, therefore, the tying of aid to specific sources can be quite harmful. It is necessary to work towards a situation where this method is not considered crucial to the preservation of a sound balance-of-payments position in the lending country. Among other measures, this will call for a greater supply of international liquidity, so that the lending countries will feel more confident of handling temporary balance-of-payments difficulties. The problem is also likely to become more manageable as more countries come to participate in the aid process. A wider distribution of both donors and recipients makes it less probable that any single donor will get into balance-of-payments difficulties – unless, of course, it is managing its economic affairs in such a fashion as to inhibit exports.

Since country-tied aid is very much a characteristic of bilateral aid (given by one country *directly* to another), it is perhaps worth considering at this stage the issues raised by the choice between *bilateral* and *multilateral* aid. Multilateral aid is channelled through *international* organisations. As of now, bilateral aid appears to be overwhelmingly preferred by the donor nations and constitutes no less than 90% of the aid flow to underdeveloped countries (see illustration 30). In fact, multilateral aid is slightly overstated in the usual statistics: half of French multilateral aid in 1960, for instance, went to the European Economic Community Development Fund for Overseas Countries and Territories; and nearly 90% of this went to former and present French colonies in Africa, so that the aid might well be considered bilateral *de facto*.

The preference of the donor countries for bilateralism is easy to appreciate. It is difficult to imagine the Soviet Union giving aid to South Vietnam; the United States is similarly unlikely to assist Red China, North Korea and Cuba. Aid is intimately and inevitably mixed up with politics. And the drawback of true multilateralism is that the politics of a country may not appeal to those who give out aid. United Nations agencies might draw upon the Soviet Union and assist Formosa and Turkey! The refusal of the Soviet Union to share the bill for the U.N. operation in the (former) Belgian Congo illustrates the political response that multilateralism typically prompts. Indeed, multilateralism is likely to be opposed even by some recipient countries. A country favoured by aid flow from an affluent partner in a political alliance (e.g. Pakistan) may well stand to lose if all aid were centrally pooled and shared out among the numerous underdeveloped recipients according to some ethical, economic and political criteria.

While bilateralism is strongly entrenched in the political realities of the international system, it is popularly supposed to have serious shortcomings. On the one hand, there is the question of 'strings' to aid. If aid is linked with politics, the recipient country may be subject to political pressures from the donor country both before and after the aid flow. True enough; but it is worth recalling the skilful way in which India, Egypt and other neutral nations have managed to keep clear of the Cold War while receiving aid from a large number of sources. Nor is the question of strings entirely prejudicial to bilateralism. Many economists, noting the wasteful use of aid in countries such as the Dominican Republic, have now come to the arguable point of view that *economic* strings *should* be attached to aid if it is to be absorbed to the recipient country's advantage. For example, an economic programme (such as a Five-Year Plan) must be a precondition of aid. In fact, such preconditions may well be more easily imposed in bilateral aid flows than through an omnibus, multilateral aid agency.

Some also fear that bilateralism may prevent the growth of progressive burden-sharing among a large number of donor countries. This view presupposes that multilateralism in *aid distribution* is necessary to a more systematic and equitable distribution of the *aid burden* itself. However, this argument is not compelling. It should be possible to divorce the two issues; indeed, since either question is politically difficult, it is perhaps more sensible not to attempt the solution of both in a single move.

The genuine limitations of bilateralism in aid lie elsewhere. To begin with, multilateralism is probably the only way of bringing aid to underdeveloped countries with no political attraction for the affluent, aid-giving nations. This in itself, however, requires only that bilateralism be partially supplemented by a multilateral distribution of some fraction of the aggregate aid flow. The other, possibly serious shortcoming of bilateralism is that the exact

Figure 30. *Estimated net inflow of long-term capital into underdeveloped countries: percentage shares of bilateral and multilateral aid, 1951–61.* The proportion of multilateral inflow is still insignificant.

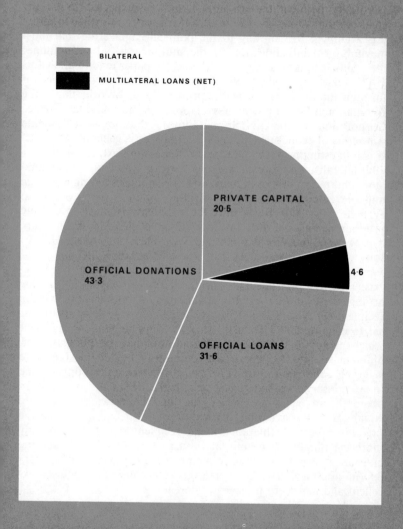

distribution of aid among the recipient countries will follow an essentially political pattern and cannot be expected to fit any ideal economic or ethical format. Yet it is open to cynics to refute this argument by pointing to the political engineering that must inevitably attend allocation in the multilateral aid programme: the reality is harsher than ideal schemes on paper tend to allow for.

The relatively modest role of multilateral assistance (dispensed through international agencies: principally the World Bank, the International Development Association, the International Finance Corporation and the U.N. Special Fund) is thus not as unfortunate – in terms of economic efficiency or equity as is generally thought. It is interesting however that, in a different context, the notion of multilateralism in foreign aid has recently come to be adopted more and more. It is customary now for countries aiding a specific underdeveloped country to get together into a *consortium*, and to evaluate their aid efforts plus the recipient country's economic programme *in toto*. For instance, there is the Aid India Club, consisting of the World Bank and West Germany, U.K., U.S.A., Italy, France, Canada, Austria, the Netherlands, Belgium, and Japan, which co-ordinates the aid flow to India. Similar consortia exist also for Pakistan and Turkey. These are essentially *ad hoc* arrangements and have many advantages for both donors and the recipient. They save the recipient the need to repeat its appeal for aid to each donor. They also permit a simultaneous arrangement which facilitates the efficient allocation of aid for imports from different sources. Perhaps most important, they enable the more generous countries to bring pressure at consortium meetings on the more conservative aid-givers and persuade them to be more liberal. From the point of view of the donor countries, consortia are equally useful in avoiding duplication of effort and in making the pre-aid, overall evaluation of the recipient country's economy more meaningful. The multilateral aspect also tends to make the assistance programme of each member country of the consortium *appear* apolitical. For these reasons, the consortium idea is excellent and has every prospect of spreading.

Two other aspects of foreign aid are of importance and have recently been widely discussed. They concern the problem of *repayment* and the question of longer-period commitments in aid flow to the underdeveloped countries.

It is easy enough to see that an efficient use of both foreign and domestic resources can be made only if these can be reasonably estimated for some length of time. If a large volume of aid were available in one year but dried up unexpectedly in the next, the plans of the recipient country could be seriously upset. This factor has led underdeveloped countries to stress the importance of having 'commitments' over longer periods than a year. In principle, of course, the period over which commitments may be made should be quite long: that a perspective view of the economy is necessary for effective and efficient planning has already been emphasised earlier (chapter 14). In practice, however, *formal* commitments are unlikely to be forthcoming for anything over two or three years. But in so far as the period *can* be stretched by national governments in the advanced countries, the effectiveness of the aid flow will ·be increased.

The question of repayments is equally ticklish. Aid is divided into outright grants and long-period loans. The latter have to be repaid; and they also carry interest. These liabilities gradually mount up and, as time passes, begin to cut into the recipient country's export receipts. This can be a serious problem unless the country can step up its foreign exchange earnings to handle these payments *plus* its import requirements. In practice, the problem has been alarming: in Turkey, for example, the burden of repayments and interest on foreign aid during the 1950's has amounted to nearly a third of Turkish export earnings during the 1963–67 Plan.

In the long run, the solution lies in a reformed international trade mechanism which will promote a rapid expansion of exports from the underdeveloped countries. In the perspective of the next two decades, however, two remedies exist: 1 a shift to more grants and fewer loans; and 2 loans with 'softer' terms. In fact, however the trend has been away from grants and towards loans! Fortunately, the loans have been getting 'softer' in many instances, especially from the United States. U.S. loans are now generally repayable in local currencies (which gets round the question of finding the foreign exchange for repayment) or carry nominal rates of interest and have tremendously long duration. The loans from Japan, Italy and West Germany have not been comparably soft, although the interest rates charged have been somewhat lower than the commercial, market rates. In fact, over 30% of the bilateral, long-term loans to underdeveloped countries during 1961 had a maturity period of twenty years or more. It is to be hoped that this trend towards softer loans will continue.

There is just one further aspect of official capital transfers to underdeveloped countries which we must consider. This relates to what is described as 'commodity aid'. Under its Public Law 480 programme, the United States has been sending surplus agricultural commodities to the developing countries by way of aid. During 1956–61 alone, such aid amounted to nearly $1·6 billion. It consisted primarily of wheat but also covered long-staple cotton and other commodities. The procedure involves the 'sale' of these commodities to recipient governments for local currencies. These currency balances, called *counterpart funds*, are technically available for spending by the U.S. government in the recipient country. In practice, however, either they have been substantially cut down by transfer to the recipient government in the nominal guise of grant 'funds for projects' or they have been allowed to accumulate unspent at an alarming rate (as in India). In either case, the result has been to make the PL 480 'sale' a *de facto* grant.

This form of aid has certain drawbacks, of course. For instance, it amounts to strait-jacketing the form in which aid flows to the underdeveloped countries. This may be undesirable because these countries may prefer to have aid instead for imports of capital goods and raw materials. There is also the more serious criticism that the PL 480 programme inhibits the development of agriculture in the recipient countries. This may be correct in a factual

A general view of the £120,000,000 Durgapur Steelworks, in West Bengal, showing the blast-furnaces and cooling-towers – an example of project-tied aid.

sense but it is *not* alarming. If the recipient country gets wheat through PL 480, it may produce less wheat itself. But the resources released this way can be used for *other* purposes. Thus, a steel mill may be put up from the foreign exchange released because a few fertiliser factories can be dropped now that less wheat has to be produced. This in turn will mean that more steel will be available in the future from domestic production. Thus, in the future, even if the PL 480 programme disappears from the international scene, the recipient country need not be brought to disaster: its agricultural demand can then be satisfied by increased imports, using the foreign exchange released by the reduction in steel imports made possible by increased steel production. The economic loss, to be subtracted from the gains from aid, accrues only in so far as the recipient country could have gained more income by increasing agricultural rather than steel production. More agricultural expansion would also mean, for most overpopulated, underdeveloped countries, a faster elimination of underemployment and a slowing down of the explosive emigration to cities.

However, against these shortcomings as regards the recipient countries, we must reckon the fact that the cost of such aid to the United States is negligible. The commodities are in surplus, generated by farm-support programmes; in terms of alternatives foregone, the aid is practically costless. It is also a type of aid which is likely to expand as other affluent countries, such as France, begin to accumulate surpluses behind high tariff walls.

Private foreign investment

The role of *private* foreign investment in the process of assisting the developing countries raises three separate questions: 1 Is such investment acceptable to the underdeveloped countries? 2 If so, is it likely to be forthcoming in substantial amounts? 3 Can anything be done to improve the terms at which these countries can attract foreign capital?

In the years after the Second World War, as countries successively became independent in Asia, Africa and the Middle East, it was evident that their attitude towards foreign investment was inevitably coloured by their colonial past. But the passage of time has changed the situation strikingly in practically all underdeveloped areas. The change is indeed so impressive that these nations now appear to be actively engaged in competing for the funds that flow annually to the underdeveloped world.

The total volume of such private capital flow, however, has

expanded little in the last two decades. As remarked earlier (in chapter 5), this deceleration originated in the reduced significance of the extractive industries which attracted so much private investment in the underdeveloped regions in the nineteenth century. Today, however, it is reinforced by essentially political worries: of nationalisation, confiscation and punitive economic legislation.

To counter these fears, the developing countries have recently been offering a wide variety of inducements to foreign investors. These consist typically of tax rebates, other discriminatory tax benefits, guarantees against nationalisation and formal commitments to permit repatriation of profits. The situation that has developed is one of *unhealthy* competition among the underdeveloped countries, resulting frequently in mutually offsetting action which is of benefit only to the foreign investors. There is clearly a pressing need for the developing countries to agree among themselves on a *common code*, which would co-ordinate and match the various advantages they hold out to prospective investors. International co-operation in disseminating information on the profitability of investment in the underdeveloped countries *in general* is also necessary. Such action would be usefully supplemented if the advanced countries themselves acted to alleviate the fears of their nationals by, for instance, introducing insurance schemes against the risks of nationalisation and blocked repatriation of profits – a measure which the United States government has been operating for some time.

The attempts to attract private foreign investment have led not only to an excessive granting of privileges. They have also prompted certain *types* of concessions which are inimical to the long-term interests of the underdeveloped countries. Prominent among these is the sanction sometimes accorded to clauses preventing third-market sales. A French radio firm may invest in an Indonesian radio plant but rule out the export of these radios to South Asia – so that French radio exports are not jeopardised. Such restrictions obviously cut into the prospects for increasing Indonesian exports. India has had a good deal of experience of these practices; and its government has rightly forbidden such clauses to be inserted in future agreements about foreign investment. In fact, since the remittance of profits on private investment can lead to a sizeable drain on a country's foreign exchange earnings, the under-developed countries may find it profitable to go even further and put pressure on foreign investors to export a certain proportion of their annual production. The Indian government, again, have recently been reasonably successful in doing this with the majority of their foreign investors. Once again, such policies are likely to be more successful if they are undertaken by a majority of the under-developed countries.

However, even with all possible reforms in the framework governing the flow of private capital, few analysts expect the size of these investments to increase so significantly as to make it unnecessary to step up official capital transfers during the next three decades. Indeed, foreign aid is so crucial to the prospects for *rapid* economic expansion in the underdeveloped areas that reforms in its pattern and procedures of disbursement and increase in its magnitude have a compelling urgency.

24 Sharing the know-how

The international transfer of resources involves also the transmission of technical expertise: in the shape of *both* blueprints *and* skilled manpower. The importance of such transfers is underlined by the rising trend in the funds disbursed by Technical Aid agencies, the increasing number of private technical collaboration agreements and the growing practice of combining technical assistance with foreign aid.

As with capital, techniques and personnel move from the advanced to the developing countries in three ways: 1 multilateral, official programmes; 2 bilateral, official programmes; and 3 private arrangements. Among the official programmes, the role of multilateral assistance is limited to about 6% of the total official expenditure on technical aid (refer back to figure 17). The quantitative magnitude of technical assistance, however, is impossible to assess meaningfully. Such assistance ranges from educational exchange programmes and supply of blueprints (neither of which may be reflected in expenditure totals) to the 'breaking-in' of a new plant by foreign technicians and by training programmes in parent companies. In any case the essential questions here concern the *quality* of these international transfers.

Transfer of skilled manpower

These questions are particularly relevant to the flow of technical people to the underdeveloped areas. This flow occurs either at the purely governmental level (e.g. the Technical Co-operation Mission of the United States), or at the international agency level (e.g. the United Nations Expanded Programme of Technical Assistance) or at the private level (e.g. Ford Foundation grants and technical personnel sent by private, foreign investors). The problems that it raises are, however, more or less the same.

The most striking difficulties that have attended these international transfers can be traced *either* to the limited intellectual equipment of the 'experts' *or* to their superficial understanding of the problems of the underdeveloped countries which they visit *or* to

225

their inadequate appreciation of the uneasy relationship that frequently exists between a foreign adviser and his client.

The technical incompetence of visiting experts sponsored under assistance programmes presents a problem which is largely unsolvable. It stems fundamentally from the limited supply of competent people, especially for work in the underdeveloped areas. There are, however, two ways in which the present situation can be improved. In the first place, a larger number of professional institutions should begin to create interest in such work among their members. Since the problem is partly due to ignorance on the part of both the sponsoring agencies and professional personnel, the whole procedure of recruitment should be institutionalised. A useful example has been set in this direction by such schemes as the American Economic Association's proposed roster of economists available for overseas work and the Development Advisory Service of the World Bank. Secondly, it is necessary to be ruthlessly selective in appointments to advisory assignments. Most programme directors believe today in putting up with 'anything that is available'. This may sound attractive: the best should not be allowed to be the enemy of the good. And yet, experience points the other way. In most professions, anything short of a good performance can be disastrous. A bad engineer can bust a dam; a poor economist will waste valuable foreign exchange assistance. There is also nothing more irritating than an incompetent foreign expert, living in comfort and putting on the airs of his high office without having anything to justify them at all. Experience in Pakistan, for instance, with foundation-sponsored, visiting economists, and in Turkey with many experts sent by international organisations has shown that such assistance brings a good deal of dissatisfaction and no gain. Why spend so much foreign aid on incompetence? The underdeveloped countries would benefit far more if the funds were merely given to them by way of straightforward capital inflow!

The problem of how to acquaint visitors with the actual conditions of the country is easier to solve. Long-period assignments are clearly likely to be more fruitful than ones lasting three or four months. The latter even encourage sketchy and offhand advice which can sometimes be quite disastrous – as in the case of certain peripatetic economists from universities whose vacations usually define the length of their stay in the countries advised! These experts also frequently tend to bring with them modes of analysis more suited to their own countries. American engineers, for example, are prone to automation and have to guard against equating mechanisation with efficiency in overpopulated countries with abundant labour. Long-period terms and careful, preliminary

Leprosy, one of the most ancient of diseases, is now confined almost entirely to tropical and sub-tropical areas. Here, at the town dispensary of Maroua, in the Cameroons, a little boy holds his record card behind his back, as he waits for his weekly ration of disulone tablets.

study of the social, economic and other facets of the country of assignment are two respects in which the transmission of professional expertise to the underdeveloped areas can be reshaped to immense advantage.

Not all of these difficulties apply to the technical personnel sent out by foreign investors in underdeveloped countries. The operation of the profit motive can be relied on to ensure the choice of suitable and competent staff, for adequately long periods. Their efficiency, however, will certainly vary with the knowledge they acquire of the conditions in the underdeveloped country and their ability to adjust to them.

An important problem of choice arises in connection with the use of expertise coming under these various arrangements. It is also a choice not always understood by the recipient country or by the directors of assistance programmes. Take medical aid, for example. If a team of doctors were sent for a short spell, under a WHO programme, to Zanzibar, they could certainly alleviate much distress *immediately*. But, if they were used instead in a medical college, they could assist crucially in building up the institution so as to produce a greater annual flow of Zanzibar doctors *in the future*. The choice here is similar to the class of long-period v. short-period choices we have discussed extensively earlier (chapter 11). It is also the choice which many aiding agencies, unappreciative of the long-run implications, readily make in favour of the short-period solution. Once this is understood, it is also easy to make economic sense of the policy of imposing *indigenous recruitment quotas* on foreign enterprises. It is certainly true that this is inefficient from the short-term point of view; but it undoubtedly builds up local skills over a period.

This, in fact, is an argument that many underdeveloped countries themselves are prone to forget in other contexts. In India, for example, there was initially great difficulty in securing designing and other contracts for indigenous engineering and consultant firms. Often fears of inefficiency arising from inexperience were exaggerated; and no weight was assigned to the inexperience of

foreign firms in working under local conditions. This naturally inhibited the growth of indigenous talent. The policy was most dramatically reversed in the case of the Bokaro steel plant, whose designing contract was assigned to a local consultant firm which in fact gave excellent performance at *lower* cost than foreign firms.

Blueprints and techniques

A considerable transmission of techniques and blueprints has also developed since the Second World War. This raises somewhat different questions from those relevant to the movement of skilled manpower, although these two varieties of transfer are often linked in assistance programmes and private investments.

The bulk of these questions relate, not to the assistance linked with official aid, but to the private *technical collaboration agreements* which have mushroomed recently. These agreements cover the *sale* of technical know-how, patents and initial assistance in manufacture to local firms. They are thus tantamount to international trade in technical knowledge, and have an important role to play in extending the technical horizons of the underdeveloped countries.

However, the underdeveloped countries have to guard against certain aspects of such agreements – which may well be of advantage to the local firm, without bringing corresponding gain to the country itself. This applies typically to contracts which are designed merely to buy goodwill (e.g. a good brand name) which has no equivalent technical worth. It also holds for agreements which have generous remittance clauses, especially when related to sales turnover instead of profits earned: these will create excessive strain on the balance-of-payments position of the country.

In such cases, the cost of the purchase of technical know-how may outweigh the social benefits. Underdeveloped countries would thus be well advised to subject such agreements to careful scrutiny and *not* to encourage them regardless of their specific contents.

25 Adjustments in the network of world trade and payments

Measures to increase and improve the quality of the flow of resources to underdeveloped areas are desirable and necessary. But they cannot be adequate in themselves.

Many of these countries would like to be able to stand on their own feet eventually. This itself calls for adjustments in the network of international trade and payments. For instance, the framework of the international economy must be changed to permit exports from the developing countries to be built up rapidly. Import requirements can then be paid for largely from their own resources and relatively less from foreign aid.

But these adjustments are required not merely as an eventual substitute for transfers of resources. They can also *supplement* these transfers in the process of development itself.

These adjustments relate principally to three major areas: 1 level of export earnings; 2 instability of export earnings; and 3 international co-ordination of production and trade policies.

Expansion of export earnings

Export earnings from the underdeveloped countries can be increased by a variety of measures. However, they presuppose changes both in patterns of national behaviour and in international institutions. There has recently been much discussion at either level – the United Nations Conference on World Trade and Development at Geneva in mid-1964 representing the most impressive event in this field. However, the general consensus in favour of the required changes has not been matched so far by concrete action.

At the *national* level, these changes relate primarily to three aspects of economic policy in the advanced countries: tariffs, import quotas and revenue taxes.

The tariff policy of several high-income countries is characterised by relatively high duties on imports of finished goods and lower rates, if any, on semi-finished goods and raw materials. This practice has historical origins. It reflects the nineteenth-century pattern of political economy. The political dominance of the European

231

countries and the exclusive dependance of the colonial countries on primary exports combined to make this tariff policy advantageous to the imperialist powers, *and* feasible. In the context of contemporary international politics and economic needs, the system is archaic. It inhibits the growth of exports of new manufactures from the underdeveloped areas, by protecting excessively the domestic industries of the affluent countries against foreign competition. [Even identical tariff rates on a raw material and the finished product will protect the domestic industry. Assume, for example, that $100 is the cost of imported raw material and $200 the price of the imported finished product ($100 thus being the value added, which may be assumed common to *both* internal and foreign production). A 10% duty on each would mean that the imported cost of the raw material would rise to $110. $100 being the value added, the *domestic* cost of producing the finished product would then be $210. On the other hand, the 10% duty on *import* of the finished product raises its cost to $220. Thus the internal production of the finished product is made advantageous by an identical duty on raw materials and finished products. This will be even more advantageous when the former are more highly taxed, as is frequently the case.]

The removal of such tariff discrimination would undoubtedly promote expansion of the exports of the underdeveloped countries – as would a general reduction of the tariff on products likely to be exported by them. However, the role of tariffs is not dominant in the modern world. A large number of countries prefer to protect their industries with *import quotas*. This is the case even with countries in strong balance-of-payments positions. Thus one should also condemn the ease with which some of the advanced countries have clamped down restrictive quotas on the exports of the underdeveloped countries (as in the case of the highly restrictive quota on the import of Indian sewing machines imposed by West Germany a few years ago). These practices, by introducing the possibility of sudden loss of markets cultivated at great expense, impair the incentives of producers in the underdeveloped countries to sell abroad

Revenue duties, either on imports or on domestic sales, have also sometimes hampered the growth of markets for the underdeveloped countries. This has been the case with many tropical products. Fortunately, however, recent experience in removing these duties has been more successful than with the undesirable tariff and quota policies of the advanced countries. The relentless focus on the issue by several international organisations, combined with the absence of domestic producer lobbies (in temperate, high-income countries), has led to a gradual reduction – occasionally even to the elimination – of such duties. One of the more striking instances recently was the decision of the European Common Market to abolish levies on tea.

However, while the advanced countries can be exhorted to revise their traditional use of tariffs, quotas and revenue duties to the advantage of the underdeveloped countries, experience shows that nothing short of the *institutionalisation* of the required code of conduct will do. Such institutionalisation is, in fact, required over a much wider range of issues than we have touched on so far.

As of today, the principal trade-regulating institution happens to be the *General Agreement on Trade and Tariffs*, which enforces on its members a set of rules concerning tariffs, quotas, subsidies and other aspects of trade policy. The GATT was established after the war, and reflects the political dominance of the Western countries. It is thus out of tune *both* with the fundamentally different problems raised by the growth of underdeveloped countries *and* with their frequent adoption of the forms of economic organisation found in the Soviet Union and other socialist countries.

Among the principal changes necessary in the GATT, from the point of view of the developing countries, we must reckon those relating to 1 the subsidisation of exports; 2 the reciprocity of tariff reduction; 3 the attitude to State trading; and 4 the admission of preferential entry of the products of developing countries into the advanced countries.

The GATT rules can be stretched to allow the subsidisation of exports (Article XVIII), subject to retaliatory action on the ground of market disruption and as an anti-dumping measure. But there is hardly the kind of sanction for export subsidisation that is necessary today. And, in practice, most developing countries resort to several types of underhand subsidy, while always remaining uncertain whether the retaliatory clauses of the GATT will be invoked against them. It is necessary to revise the GATT articles in this respect. This necessity stems from two major factors. 1 There is need for the protection of 'infant industries'. Many of the new exporting industries in the developing countries happen to be in this category and fully merit assistance by way of tax rebates, production subsidies and such other measures. 2 *Export* subsidies, on the other hand, can be justified in other ways. The foreign markets are riskier to individual exporters than domestic markets; exports are therefore likely to be undervalued by individuals in relation to their social value. This undervaluation also springs from the lack of information about foreign markets relative to domestic sales possibilities. *Export* subsidies would offset such undervaluation and bring social advantage.

The GATT also needs revision so as to recognise explicitly the facts of 1 State trading and 2 the inability of the underdeveloped countries to offer reciprocal tariff concessions to the advanced countries. Articles of the GATT on these issues are strikingly out of date. With many underdeveloped countries adopting the policy of nationalised trade (e.g. Burma) or having State trading corporations to handle some fraction of trade (e.g. India), the rules of the GATT must take greater cognisance of the legitimacy and importance of these institutions, and the attendant practice of trade agreements, and cease to look upon these forms of trading as *declassé*. The tariff reduction process, around which many GATT regulations are based, has little meaning in the context of trade between two State trading agencies! It is also necessary to rewrite the clauses which insist, with rare exceptions, on reciprocity in tariff cuts. The developing countries, working frequently with planned utilisation of foreign exchange and hence with import controls, have little to offer by way of reciprocity when asking for concessions from the advanced countries. Fortunately, this fact has been appreciated more and more recently.

This is not the case, however, with the question of preferential entry for the exports of developing countries. This would call for an amendment of Article 1 of the GATT. It is also one of the most ticklish issues facing the advanced countries. The preference would consist in charging a lower duty if the commodity is imported from an underdeveloped country. Where quotas are used, the preference could take the form of the reservation of a *minimum* share for imports from the developing countries. These proposals, supported by many underdeveloped countries, are fraught with political difficulties.

Even if conceded by advanced countries, the preferences would be hard to negotiate; they may well turn out to be nominal or apparent. Moreover, the negotiations are likely to create dissensions among the underdeveloped countries themselves. There has indeed been a foretaste of such an eventuality in the demands aired by some particularly underdeveloped countries for preferences in relation to other, 'richer' underdeveloped countries! The question is further complicated by the existence of such preferences for a *few* underdeveloped countries (e.g. the Associated Overseas Territory countries of Africa *vis-à-vis* the European Common Market); these countries may well be against the spread of such preferences to yet other countries, to their own disadvantage. In fact, political considerations could well strengthen these tendencies to divisiveness: it may be natural, for instance, for the French authorities to worry more about their ex-colonies in Africa and to reinforce their existing preferential advantages.

Perhaps the most formidable opposition is likely to come from the producers' lobbies in the advanced countries. Fears of disruption in economic activity and reduction in the level of employment can be easily aroused and are traditionally powerful weapons in the fight for protection from foreign competition. Such fears can certainly, in this instance, be countered at an intellectual level without much difficulty. 1 The success of the underdeveloped

Figure 31. *Time profile of export earnings and import payments for a hypothetical country.* Countries, like individuals, do not find their payments and earnings fully synchronised. They thus have periods of surplus and deficit even if, over longer periods. they may break even. During periods of deficit, they must have resources to settle their liabilities. For this purpose, they maintain 'reserves' of internationally acceptable media such as gold.

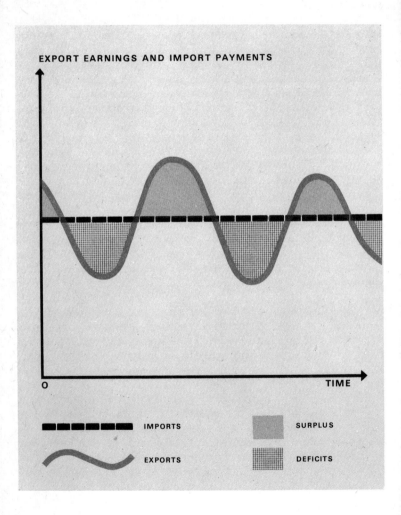

EXPORT EARNINGS AND IMPORT PAYMENTS

TIME

O

IMPORTS

EXPORTS

SURPLUS

DEFICITS

countries in exporting to the advanced countries will *not* detract from the total demand for the goods of the advanced countries. After all, the increased earnings will be spent on imports of machinery, semi-finished goods and components from the advanced countries themselves. 2 The rate at which exports of the underdeveloped countries can rise even under the most optimistic assumptions will not be large enough to cause any major adjustment problems in the expanding economies of the advanced countries. 3 Even if it were, the underdeveloped countries have always offered to negotiate in difficult cases and arrange, where necessary, for an easing of the situation by voluntarily imposing export quotas and the like. 4 Finally, the advanced countries themselves would be wise to set up machinery to facilitate the transfer of labour to expanding industries from those in decline. It is cheaper to spend resources on such activity (so as to be able to handle adjustments whenever necesary) than to be unduly frightened of disruption from foreign competition, to prevent the exports of the developing countries from growing and then to be pressured into granting additional aid! Yet valid and persuasive though such arguments are, the political opposition to them is great. It is only to be hoped that they will gain the needed support.

Instability of export earnings

The expansion of export earnings, even if successful, would not in itself alleviate the difficulties which arise from their instability. Further adjustments in the international economy are needed.

The simplest remedy is to allow countries better access to short-term credits to tide over the temporary balance-of-payments deficits which unstable export earnings imply. If the problem is genuinely one of instability, rather than of long-term deterioration in the earnings position, it should be sufficient for the country to be able to borrow during the lean, deficit periods and to repay with the foreign exchange earned during the surplus periods (as would be the case in figure 31).

This function of supplying international 'liquidity' to countries with instability in their international accounts is currently being performed by the International Monetary Fund. The IMF lends to member countries in temporary balance-of-payments difficulties. And, although the formal clauses governing borrowing are fairly stringent and dilatory, the underdeveloped countries have recently found the Fund easily approachable and readily accommodating. This has not meant, of course, *automatic* grant of credits to the borrowing countries. The Fund has been a generally sympathetic lender but it has retained its rights to adjudicate, admonish and even refuse credits.

This has led some underdeveloped countries to demand that the Fund should issue credit automatically. Thus, for example, it has been argued that any fall in a country's export earnings below the preceding three years' average should entitle the country to get automatic, compensatory short-term credit. It is unlikely, however, that such schemes will ever get the approval of the Fund (or of the creditor countries which are ultimately enabling the Fund to lend to the borrowers). And it is perhaps right that this is so. The rationale of short-term credits is that the balance-of-payments difficulty is temporary. Automatic credit would imply that those who seek to borrow will always be in genuinely short-term difficulties – a presumption that is unlikely to be conceded by the lenders and, if granted, may well turn out to be false in too many cases for the scheme to be continued.

Instead of asking for such unreasonable procedures, the underdeveloped countries would be wiser to work for expansion of the Fund's lending resources. This is necessary not merely because their own borrowing capacities need to be increased with the expansion of their trade. It is also required to meet the generally increased demand for liquidity in many *advanced* countries as well. The insufficiency of international reserves (e.g. gold), claimed by many advanced countries today, has led to serious concern about their balances of payments. And this has been responsible for inadequate response to the export efforts of the developing countries, for tying

Figure 32. *Demand schedule for a hypothetical commodity*. It shows the various quantities of the commodity which will be demanded in the market at different prices. At price OP_1, the quantity demanded is OT_1. At price OP_2, the quantity demanded is OT_2.

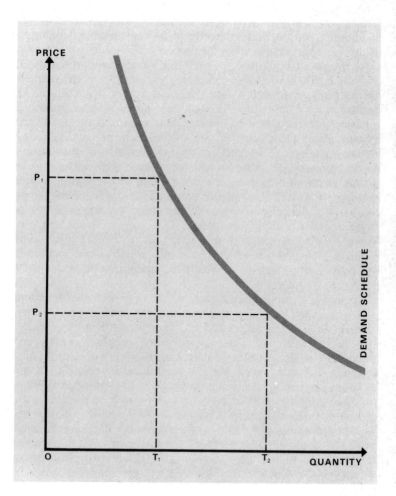

of aid and other attitudes and actions which have seriously impaired the reform of the international economy in the interests of the developing countries. Expansion of short-term borrowing facilities at the Fund, by alleviating this widespread shortage of liquidity, would thus indirectly bring considerable benefits to the underdeveloped countries themselves.

Alternatives to expansion of the Fund's resources and members' drawing rights have also been actively explored in recent years. It has been suggested that a supra-national, central bank should be created which would annually inject fresh doses of an international currency into the world economy. Other variations on this theme have also been recommended. *Any* of these schemes, adding to the liquidity available to *both* underdeveloped and advanced countries, would be beneficial to the former and deserves general support.

This entire approach to the question of instability of export earnings, however, rests on the presumption that it is enough to counter the deleterious *effects* of instability on the balances of payments of developing countries. But many analysts have preferred to devise measures to reduce the instability itself. The problem, looked at this way, becomes substantially one of *stabilising* the commodity markets in which the underdeveloped countries happen to be interested.

Commodity stabilisation schemes have been discussed time and again; and they have also been experimented with in certain commodities such as wheat, tea and tin. They raise numerous political and economic problems; and it is difficult to see them as providing an effective solution to the problems of instability in international accounts. Let us examine some of the difficulties raised by them.

To do this, we must distinguish between 1 stabilisation of earnings and 2 price stabilisation. The stabilisation of the price of a commodity can, in fact, be detrimental to the stability of earnings. Thus, for example, if the *supply* of a commodity fluctuates, a stable price will imply unstable earnings. On the other hand, if the price were allowed to fall when supply increased and to rise when it decreased, this would *reduce* instability in earnings (see figure 32, where earnings remain stable at $OP_1 \times OT_1 = OP_2 \times OT_2$ although supply changes from OT_1 to OT_2). However, when the cause of instability is *demand* fluctuations, prices and earnings will tend to fluctuate together. Thus where demand rises, given a certain supply, the resulting increase in prices will mean increased earnings. And a fall in demand will imply reduced earnings. Price stabilisation in such cases will thus be similar to income stabilisation.

Since the developing countries are interested in stabilising their exchange earnings, action is needed primarily in the case of those commodities where *demand* fluctuations, are frequent. In these cases, the establishment of *buffer stocks* has been proposed. These would permit the international agency (in charge of stabilising operations) to intervene in the market, selling when prices rise and buying when they fall unduly. The difficulty with this apparently simple scheme springs from the fixation of the average level at which prices (and earnings) are to be stabilised. This issue typically divides the producers and the consumers. The scheme can also create long-term difficulties. By maintaining average prices high through buffer-stock operations, such schemes can prevent the primary producers from getting out of *declining markets* until the question has become more complex to solve. Supporting such declining markets would also entail continuing purchases by the international agency, calling for unduly large funds. The holding of the required buffer stocks is also an expensive operation owing to the tying up of capital, normal wastage from stocks and storage charges. It is thus necessary to ask whether these direct and indirect costs attendant on buffer-stock operations aimed at commodity stabilisation are worth incurring.

Indeed, given these drawbacks, it appears more sensible to rely on schemes for expansion of international liquidity to meet the problems raised by instability than to attempt commodity stabilisation schemes. Increased access to short-term credit would, on the other hand, merely ease the *balance-of-payments* situation of the developing countries suffering from instability.

It would need to be supplemented by *domestic* measures to

offset the effect of unstable earnings on the *producers*. Thus, for example, if Ghana suffers a decline in earnings of foreign exchange due to a reduced demand for cocoa exports, the IMF can assist with short-term credit. However, this will not in itself counter the possibly deleterious effects of the reduction of demand (and instability) on cocoa production. For this reason, many developing countries would be well advised to operate *domestic*, stabilisation schemes. This recommendation, however, dove-tails into the general prescription for avoiding serious, demand-induced price and income fluctuations in agricultural and primary markets.

International co-ordination of production planning

There is yet another area in which international action seems necessary. The attempts at import-substitution in many developing countries today have led to a situation where it could be advantageous to co-ordinate investment decisions *at an international level*. Using import controls extensively, the developing countries have frequently set up domestic industries which eliminate imports even from one another, and with mutual loss of economic efficiency. This situation could be improved if the developing countries co-ordinated their investment plans so as to avoid unnecessary duplication and assigned investments to countries where they are more profitably made. Such co-ordination would naturally have to be reflected in trade agreements which ensure that 1 what is produced is exported, and 2 what is imported can be paid for from export earnings.

This issue has come up also in relation to the problem of 'economies of scale'. In many developing countries, the domestic market alone is too small for economic production to be undertaken in many industries. Thus, if each country tries to meet its various requirements entirely by domestic production, each country will have unduly high costs of production in all the industries where economies in large-scale production obtain. It would be more sensible, therefore, to have a co-ordinated plan under which each country would have a different set of industries assigned to it, and the demand for a product in *all* member countries would be satisfied from production in a single country. Thus, for example, Kenya would produce machine tools, Tanganyika radios and Nyasaland plastics – for the *entire* region. This would permit the attainment of scale-economies in each industry and the entire group of participating countries would benefit from such co-ordination. This has begun to be appreciated in many regional arrangements, such as the Common Market of the Latin American countries.

The important role that such co-ordination of investment can play in increasing the efficiency of national programmes for development therefore needs to be appreciated by the developed countries. And its implications for trade (e.g. the possible justification for bilateral and preferential trade arrangements) must be grasped, rather than rejected on the basis of arguments of an earlier period.

26 The tight-rope to progress

What then are we to conclude about the prospects for rapid transformation of the underdeveloped economies?

Economic progress is certainly not easy to engineer. The planners in the underdeveloped countries face an uphill task. They will have to understand fully the many economic, social and political factors which must condition and shape their action if it is to succeed. This will need not merely expertise but insight and imagination.

A challenge, no less great, faces the advanced countries. We have explored the innumerable ways in which they can assist in the elimination of poverty and backwardness in the poorer countries. Their attitudes on foreign aid, technical assistance, trade and other important matters will have to be changed and adjusted to the many demands raised by the economic development of more than three continents.

The difficulties are immense. And yet, as we have seen, they are not insuperable. Even if there is a tight-rope to progress, there is hope: after all we have something to hang on to in our search for material progress of the underdeveloped world. There is evidence that the world is moving, albeit slowly, towards the attitudes and actions that development calls for.

Indeed, for the idealists among us, the challenge of development represents today the kind of invigorating stimulus for sustained action that the Soviet revolution was for progressive opinion after the First World War. This itself constitutes the surest guarantee of a continual, even though halting, transition to an international framework favourable to rapid economic growth in the underdeveloped world.

Bibliography

If a book has been published both in England and in the United States both publishers are listed, the English one being named first. Dates are of first publication.

General

There are three books which can be particularly recommended as general introductions to the subject: W. A. Lewis, *The Theory of Economic Growth*, Allen & Unwin/Irwin, 1955; A. Gerschenkron, *Economic Backwardness in Historical Perspective*, O.U.P./Harvard, 1962; and G. Myrdal, *An International Economy*, Routledge/Harper, 1956. These can be usefully supplemented by two works on the Soviet economy and methods of communist planning: R. W. Campbell, *Soviet Economic Power*, Riverside Press, Cambridge, Mass., 1962, an excellent work easily intelligible to the layman; and G. Grossman (ed.), *Value and Plan*, University of California Press, 1960, which is slightly more technical. Some valuable historical and analytical material of interest to other readers besides professional economists will also be found in three volumes of the International Economic Association: L. Dupriez (ed.), *Economic Progress*, Institut de Recherches Economiques et Sociales, Louvain, 1955; W. W. Rostow (ed.), *The Economics of Take-Off into Sustained Growth*, Macmillan/St Martin's Press, 1963; and K. Berrill (ed.), *Economic Development with Special Reference to East Asia*, Macmillan, London, 1964.

1 Poverty and income distribution

For further details on the concept of national income, see P. A. Samuelson, *Economics: An Introductory Analysis*, McGraw-Hill, 1958.

4 Production and occupational structure

For anthropological literature see especially R. Firth, *Malay Fishermen: Their Peasant Economy*, Kegan Paul/Pacific Relations, 1946; and G. Dalton, 'Traditional Production in Primitive African Economies', *Quarterly Journal of Economics*, Vol. 76 No. 3, Harvard, 1962.

5 Links with the international economy

The question of exports from the underdeveloped countries is excellently discussed in R. Nurkse, *Patterns of Trade and Development*, Blackwell/New York University Press, 1961. Some chapters in A. Cairncross, *Factors in Economic Development*, Allen & Unwin/Praeger, 1962, and parts of

A. Maizel's large work *Industrial Growth and Trade*, C.U.P., 1963, are also useful in this context. *World Economic Survey*, Part I, 1962 is a useful reference for all problems of aid and trade.

9   Sociological institutions and attitudes

On the interaction of economics and sociology, three works may be cited as of special importance: F. G. Bailey, *Caste and the Economic Frontier*, O.U.P., 1958; S. Epstein, *Economic Development and Social Change in South India*, O.U.P., 1962; and B. Hoselitz and R. Lambert, *The Role of Savings and Wealth in Southern Asia and the West*, UNESCO, Paris, 1963.

17   Revolution in agriculture

A vast literature is available, from which it is difficult to choose. But mention must be made of the excellent work of Raj Krishna on land reform; 'Agrarian reform in India: the debate on ceilings', *Economic Development and Cultural Change*, Vol. 7 No. 3, Chicago, 1959 and on the supply response of farmers to price incentives: 'Farm supply response in India-Pakistan: a case study of the Punjab region', *Economic Journal*, Vol. 73 No. 291, London, 1963. Dharam Narain's work on marketed surplus is also valuable: *Distribution of the Marketed Surplus of Agricultural Produce*, Asia Publishing House, Bombay, 1961. For information on Japanese agricultural development see an excellent paper presented at the World Food Congress, 4–18 June 1963, on *Agricultural Development in Modern Japan*, FAO commission papers.

18   Industrialisation

On industrial programming, the U.N. Report on *Formulating Industrial Development Programmes*, E.C.A.F.E., Bangkok, 1961 is a useful introduction.

19   Education and manpower training

On measurements of returns from educational expenditure there is an excellent supplement of the *Journal of Political Economy*, Vol. 20 No. 4, Chicago, 1962. See also a stimulating paper by T. Balogh and P. Streeten, 'The coefficient of ignorance', *Bulletin of the Oxford University Institute of Statistics*, Vol. 25 No. 2, 1963.

20   The choice of technology

For project analysis, K. N. Raj, *Some Economic Aspects of the Bhakra Nangal Project*, Asia Publishing House, Bombay, 1960, is illuminating.

A forthcoming work by S. Marglin on *Investment Criteria for the Public Sector* (to be published by Allen and Unwin) is also excellent.

21   Reducing the birth rate

For a detailed proposal for bonus schemes for smaller families see S. Enke, 'The gains to India from population control', *Review of Economics and Statistics*, Vol. 42 No. 2, Harvard, 1960.

22   The political economy of development

W. A. Lewis's paper in M.S. Adiseshiah (ed.), *The Restless Nations*, Allen & Unwin/Dodd, Mead, 1962 has interesting ideas on the tensions in economic development.

23   International transfer of resources

See Rosenstein-Rodan, 'International aid for underdeveloped countries', *Review of Economics and Statistics*, Vol. 43 No. 2, Harvard, 1961; I. Kravis, 'The political arithmetic of international burden-sharing', *Journal of Political Economy*, Vol. 21 No. 4, Chicago, 1963. F. Benham's *Economic Aid to Underdeveloped Countries*, O.U.P., is a useful elementary textbook. See also a stimulating article by T. Balogh and P. Streeten, 'Domestic versus foreign investment', *Bulletin of the Oxford University Institute of Statistics*, Vol. 22 No. 3, 1960.

24   Sharing the know-how

There are more valuable comments on technical collaboration agreements in 'Post-war foreign investment in India', *Economic Bulletin for Asia and the Far East*, Bangkok, Vol. 13, 1962–3.

Acknowledgments

In writing this book, I have been conscious of three sets of obligations. First, I would like to record the many insights which I derived from my term of eighteen months with the Indian Statistical Institute, in its Planning Unit at the Planning Commission of India. The economics of underdeveloped countries cannot really be understood through armchair research. My 'field research' has made me emphasise several aspects of planning which are absolutely crucial in understanding the problems and programmes of the underdeveloped countries today. Indeed, it is one of the distinguishing features of this book that it will enable the reader to understand and evaluate for himself the ever-growing development plans of the underdeveloped countries. Secondly, I have drawn frequently on the invaluable work of the United Nations, in its many agencies, for much documentation on the developing countries. Thirdly, and most of all, I would like to thank my colleagues, Padma Desai and I. G. Patel, who have gone through the manuscript and made many valuable suggestions.

My thanks are due to Mr T. Stalker-Miller who designed the maps and diagrams and to the following sources for providing information or material for adaptation: figures 1, 5–8, 18 and table 1 Norton Ginsburg, *Atlas of Economic Development*, University of Chicago Press, 1961; figure 2 G. Hanoch, *Income Differentials in Israel*, 5th Report, Falk Project, Jerusalem, 1961, p. 40; figure 3 S. Melman (ed.), *Disarmament: Its Politics and Economics*, American Academy of Arts and Science, Boston, Mass., 1962, pp. 383–92; figure 4 *The U.N. Statistical Yearbook 1962*, table 165, pp. 408–503; table 2 *World Economic Survey, 1961*, United Nations, New York, 1962, p. 18; figures 9 and 10 C. P. Kindleberger, *Economic Development*, McGraw-Hill, (the production data come originally from W. S. and E. S. Woytinsky, *World Population and Production*, Twentieth Century Fund, New York, 1953 and the per capita G.N.P. data from M. L. Watkins' calculations for 1949 for Center for International Studies, M.I.T., Cambridge, Mass.); figures 11–13 J. D. Coppock, *International Economic Instability*, McGraw-Hill, 1962; table 3 Ragnar Nurkse's Wicksell Lectures on *Patterns of Trade Development*, Basil Blackwell/O.U.P., 1961; figures 14, 15, 17 *World Economic Survey, 1962, Part I*, United Nations, New York, 1963; figure 16 and table 4 *Economic Bulletin for Asia and the Far East*, Vol. 13, No. 3, 1962; figure 19 Kingsley Davis, 'The Amazing Decline of Mortality in Underdeveloped Areas', *American Economic Review, Papers and Proceedings*, May 1956; figure 20 *U.N. Demographic Yearbook, 1953*; tables 6–9 W. Leontief, *Structure of American Economy, 1919–39*, Harvard University

250

Press/O.U.P., 1941; figure 29 adapted from a chart in an article by Julian Feiss in *Scientific American*, September 1963, p. 130; figure 30 P.N. Rosenstein-Rodan, 'International Aid for Underdeveloped Countries', *Review of Economics and Statistics*, May 1961 (the definition of aid used must be carefully noted); figure 31 I. Kravis and M. Davenport, 'The Political Arithmetic of International Burden-Sharing', *Journal of Political Economy*, August 1963; figure 32 *World Economic Survey, 1962, Part I*, p. 114.

Acknowledgment is also due to the following for the illustrations (the number refers to the page on which the illustration appears): *frontispiece* The John Hillelson Agency and Brian Brake; 8 WHO and Eric Schwab; 18, 19 Angela Hackelsberger; 27 Patrick Ward; 38 U.S. Information Services; 39, 226 U.N.; 42 FAO and Jack Ling; 50 Press Association Ltd; 52 Milton D. Macaulay; 53 Stephen Harrison; 54 Ghana Information Office; 59, 104, 194 Camera Press Ltd; 66 British Petroleum; 74 Camera Press Ltd and Paul Almasy; 81, 109, 158 Tunisian Embassy, London; 86, 97 Camera Press Ltd and John Bulmer; 90 WHO and P.N. Sharma; 91 WHO; 141, 174 Central Office of Information, London; 149 Camera Press Ltd and U.N.; 153 FAO and C. Bavagnoli; 156, 163, 177 T.S. Nagarajan; 171 Press Information Bureau, Government of India; 180 ILO; 185 © Unesco/W. Hubell 1961; 221 C.S. Services Ltd; 229 WHO and Pierre Pittet.

The quotation in chapter 10 is from Eric Stokes, *The English Utilitarians and India*, O.U.P., 1959.

J. B.

Index

252

World University Library

Some books published or in preparation

Economics and Social Studies

The World Cities
Peter Hall, *London*

The Economics of Underdeveloped Countries
Jagdish Bhagwati, *Delhi*

Development Planning
Jan Tinbergen, *Rotterdam*

Leadership in New Nations
T. B. Bottomore, *Vancouver*

Key Issues in Criminology
Roger Hood, *Durham*

The Sociology of Communication
J. L. Aranguren, *Madrid*

Education in the Modern World
John Vaizey, *Oxford*

History

Ancient Egypt
Werner Kaiser, *Berlin*

The Emergence of Greek Democracy
W. G. Forrest, *Oxford*

Mahomet and the Great Arabian Conquests
Francesco Gabrieli, *Rome*

The Crusades
G. Widengren, *Uppsala*

The Medieval Economy
Georges Duby, *Aix-en-Provence*

The Ottoman Empire
Halil Inalcik, *Ankara*

The Rise of Toleration
Henry Kamen, *Edinburgh*

The Left in Europe
David Caute, *Oxford*

Chinese Communism
Robert C. North, *Stanford*

History and Sociology of Religion

History of the Christian Church
W. O. Chadwick, *Cambridge*

Monasticism
Dom David Knowles, *London*

Judaism
Rabbi J. Soetendorp, *Amsterdam*

The Modern Papacy
K. O. von Aretin, *Göttingen*

Sects
Bryan Wilson, *Oxford*

Language and Literature

A Model of Language
E. M. Uhlenbeck, *Leyden*

French Literature
Raymond Picard, *Sorbonne*

Russian Literature
Ronald Hingley, *Oxford*

Satire
Matthew Hodgart, *Sussex*

The Arts

Primitive Art
Eike Haberland, *Mainz*

The Language of Modern Art
Ulf Linde, *Stockholm*

Aesthetic Theories since 1850
J. F. Revel, *Paris*

Art Nouveau
S. T. Madsen, *Oslo*

Academic Painting
Gerald Ackerman, *Stanford*

Palaeolithic Art
P. J. Ucko and A. Rosenfeld, *London*

Modern Drama
Peter Szondi, *Göttingen*

Psychology and Human Biology

Eye and Brain
R. L. Gregory, *Cambridge*

The Ear and the Brain
Edward Carterette, *U.C.L.A.*

The Variety of Man
J. P. Garlick, *London*

The Biology of Work
O. G. Edholm, *London*

Bioengineering
H. S. Wolff, *London*

Psychoses
H. J. Bochnik, *Hamburg*

Child Development
Philippe Muller, *Neuchâtel*

Man and Disease
Gernot Rath, *Göttingen*

Zoology and Botany

Animal Communication
N. Tinbergen and J. M. Cullen, *Oxford*

Mimicry
Wolfgang Wickler, *Starnberg*

Migration
Gustaf Rudebeck, *Stockholm*

The World of an Insect
Remy Chauvin, *Sorbonne*

Biological Rhythms
Janet Harker, *Cambridge*

Lower Animals
Martin Wells, *Cambridge*

Physical Science and Mathematics

Mathematics in Science and Daily Life
H. Freudenthal, *Utrecht*

The Physics of Low Temperatures
K. A. G. Mendelssohn, *Oxford*

Particles and Accelerators
Robert Gouiran, *C.E.R.N., Geneva*

Optics
A. C. S. van Heel, *Delft*

Waves and Corpuscles
J. A. E. Silva and G. Lochak, *Paris*
Introduction by Louis de Broglie

Earth Sciences and Astronomy

Anatomy of the Earth
André de Cayeux, *Sorbonne*

The Electrical Earth
J. Sayers, *Birmingham*

Climate and Weather
H. Flohn, *Bonn*

The Structure of the Universe
E. L. Schatzman, *Sorbonne*

Applied Science

Words and Waves
A. H. Beck, *Cambridge*

Operational Research
A. Kaufmann, *Sorbonne*